Keepers of the Story

For Eva

With Warmest Wishes, hoping these stories "speak" to you.

Tony Cowan

New Mexico
28 February '98

Also by Megan McKenna

Not Counting Women and Children: Neglected Stories from the Bible

Parables: The Arrows of God

Mary: Shadow of Grace

Angels Unawares

Lent: The Daily Readings

Lent: The Sunday Readings

Rites of Justice: The Sacraments and Liturgy as Ethical Imperatives

Keepers of the Story

Oral Traditions in Religion

───── ✳ ─────

**Megan McKenna
and
Tony Cowan**

ORBIS BOOKS
Maryknoll, New York 10545

The Catholic Foreign Mission Society of America (Maryknoll) recruits and trains people for overseas missionary service. Through Orbis Books, Maryknoll aims to foster the international dialogue that is essential to mission. The books published, however, reflect the opinions of their authors and are not meant to represent the official position of the society.

Published by Orbis Books, Maryknoll, NY 10545-0308
Manufactured in the United States of America

Biblical translations are from the *Christian Community Bible*, 17th edition (Claretian Publications, 1995).

Library of Congress Cataloging-in-Publication Data

McKenna, Megan.
    Keepers of the story : oral traditions in religion / Megan McKenna and Tony Cowan.
        p.   cm.
    Includes bibliographical references.
    ISBN 1-57075-145-5 (alk. paper)
    1. Storytelling—Religious aspects.   I. Cowan, Tony.   II. Title.
BL628.7.M34   1997
291.1'3—dc21   97-25239
                                                                            CIP

In memory of Ken Feit, itinerant fool
October 13, 1940–August 8, 1981

and
for Paul Ilecki, musician, weaver, dancer, friend
and
for Joseph and Jeffrey
who always listen to my story.

In memory of Virgil Jutai Lorenzo
Musician, Friend, and Mystic
"Somewhere, he is singing still."
(Tony Cowan)

Contents

Preface

What do you say before the words: "Once upon a time," or "In the beginning"? Anyone who tells stories, preaches, speaks in public, teaches, makes an announcement of importance, initiates a conversation with a stranger, or even just seeks communication, knows that what comes before the words is a deep, slow breath, an inspiring moment. Even more, those who have been touched or grasped by the force of words know there is a conspiracy—the breathing together of flesh and spirit, of Spirit and community, of earth and all that lives or ever has lived—in the "once-upon-a-times."

In every culture, in every geographical place, among every people, there are individuals who are entrusted with the words that belong to that place and group. They hold the heritage, the experiences, and the stories that express who they are and how they stand in the universe. These are the keepers of the Story. Their lives are dedicated to preserving, to keeping true, to guarding and protecting what is not theirs alone, but what has been given into their care by others. It is a vocation, a calling, a responsibility and a work that defines them in relation to their people and in relation to other groups and their stories. They live on the words but they never make their living from the words. The tales tell *them*. The stories use their flesh, their voices and minds, to remain alive and to keep the people alive. The keepers are given words, and are held in sway and bondage by the lifelines of hope, suffering, exaltation, births and deaths, resurrections, and visions: by the Story.

There are many keepers—storytellers, *griots*, shamans, medicine chiefs, Zen masters, *seanachaí*, monk-scribes, singers, musicians, gypsies, angels who are messengers of God, hasids and rebbes, mystics and tale-spinners—but there is only the one Story. It is a singular question in myriad forms. It is a universal pronouncement in expressions beyond numbering. It is a cry sounded in every generation, every place, and each human heart that wonders, asks, demands, whispers, shouts, chants, begs, prays and repeats again and again and again. Who are we? Who am I? Who are you? Who art Thou? Are we all one? What is truth? Are we true? Is the end in the beginning? Where are we now? What is it that sings among the stars and in our blood and in the empty places of the world and in the wolves' howling and in the human heart? This is the Story, the only Story there is to tell, to refashion and tell again. It is the only Story there is to listen to and discuss and share with others, to pass on to our children and to use as an introduction to other nations, religions, peoples, cultures. In the speaking we find our voice, we remember echoes and take heed of all that converges on us in blessings and blunders. In the hearing we are sounded, tuned and drawn into the universe—the one poem, the one verse, the one harmony, the one Holiness.

The mystery of the one Story is forever giving birth to expression, to transformation and transfiguration and redemption as we live, endure, and die. Even if the essence of the Story is wrenched from us or twisted, broken or lost, there is a fervent belief among the keepers that killing the teller only gives the Story more meaning, power and possibility. The real issue is: Do you serve? Do you obey? Does the Story seize hold of your flesh and tell you? Are you, are we, coming true? Do we believe the words that have been given to us? Do we stake our life on the words? Do the words set free and loose compassion and hope into the world? Is the Story about life, about birth, about resurrection, about passionate regard for all that has been made? Is it about tender regard, about non-violent resistance to falsehood and distortion? Is it about imagining the ending as far beyond "happily ever after"? What word are we in the Story? What will be told of us when we have become the ground of "once upon a time"?

In many ways this book is an honor to write and to share with others and I hope that the treasures of many religions and peoples that are gathered here will be reverenced and kept with integrity. I am bound to my own religious tradition and its Word made flesh, dwelling among us as justice, truth and love beyond words, but I have been given access to many other religious traditions and the richness of their words. They only serve to deepen my amazement and awe of the Story. We are all one. May we all be keepers of the Story and all come true.

Now...listen to some of the words of the Story.

Megan McKenna

Megan McKenna and Tony Cowan have recorded most of the stories that appear in *Keepers of the Story*. They are available on two 60-minute cassette tapes from Credence Cassettes, P. O. Box 419491, Kansas City, Missouri 64141-6491. Tel: 1-800-333-7373; Fax: 1-816-968-2292.

Introduction

This book has been "in the making" for about fifty-two years, a very short period of time as stories themselves go. For as long as I can remember I have played with words. I was fortunate to grow up in a family that cherished learning and in a house that was bulging with books. My father would often come home from work with a box of books he got for a dollar or two at a second-hand store—a grab-bag-collection. You never knew what treasures would be hidden below the dusty paperback mysteries and books on dog training and faraway places. Every closet was stacked with novels and in the basement early on I built a lair of books, where invariably I could be found, hiding out, alone, reading voraciously. I even read my way through high school: poetry in algebra class; novels in history; science fiction in religion; hard science in English lit; the classics on the way to gym and travelogues in especially boring classes.

It was only a matter of time before I tried my hand at my own version of poem, tales and reflections, stumbling to find a voice, a style and a truthfulness that expressed all the dreams stirred in my own soul. Words beget words as dreams beget dreams. Later I learned that silence was the best ground for growing such gorgeous creatures as stories. But I knew I was on the right track when I discovered such quotes as this from Franz Kafka: "You do not need to leave your room. Remain sitting at your table and listen. Do not even listen, simply wait. Do not even wait, be quite still and solitary. The world will freely offer itself to you to be unmasked, it has no choice. It will roll in ecstasy at your feet."

I started collecting, borrowing, stealing, chewing on words, snippets and bits that could be savored, tongued and reflected upon at leisure, brought out again and again as photographs that brought back another earlier world. The sense came quickly that words could save you, alter reality and transform the drab into something pulsing with life and possibility. So I started what I call my "Quote Books" where I collected the world in pieces of alphabet and script.

Here is a piece from a very "old" book, cut out and pasted in my "Quote Book" when I was "very young." Unfortunately, I have no idea who wrote it, or where it was born...but it's too good not to share.

> When I was born an old man appeared to me and said, "I am going to give you a present. I am going to give you a hole. I keep the hole safe in my left ear and I am going to break off a piece of that hole and give it to you for a present. You keep it in your left ear. Any time you come to a situation where there is no exit—concrete floor, concrete ceiling, concrete walls—remember the gift that I've given you. Take that hole out of your ear and go to the nearest wall and, as hard as you can, throw the hole against that wall and there'll be a hole in the wall. Put your mouth to it and call and hole will call to hole, and I will hear you and I will get you out.

In no time at all I was hopelessly enthralled by words, so it is not surprising that all of my good friends, mentors and kinfolk of the spirit, were equally in love with stories and words. It served as our common language, a springboard and life-line across continents, and eventually to every corner of the universe. I am indebted in this book to a litany of folk so long that the names can't really be included, except for a few that scream for remembrance.

This book is dedicated to Ken Feit, itinerant fool and preacher, who first painted my face white, looked hard at me, smiled and said: Now say it all without even one word! And equally there are thanks rendered to Paul Ilecki, musician and weaver and lover of mystery who gave me a coat of many colors, full of great pockets (homes for bubbles, my puppets and balloons, etc.) and made me a clown and performer, dancer and storyteller. My gratitude to Chris Witt for his story of "The Water-Carrier" and to John Donaghy for his many testimonies and transcribed recordings from El Salvador, and so many others who give me stories on scraps of paper.

But this book would never have made it from hope and a bundle of words into enfleshed stories and written form without my friend and fellow-storyteller, musician, composer and weaver of words, Tony Cowan, who has given me so many of his stories to be used here for the first time in print. Such gifts are beyond price. Such soul-friends are rare in any life. And so, this introduction begins with a story that reveals the depth of what stories are, their power and conception, their generation and magic. It follows the first rule of storytelling as I always begin: All stories are true; some of them actually happened. This one actually happened, halfway across a world, to Tony. It will set the stage and hopefully draw all of you into this book and deeper into the world of words, and the Word made flesh. It is called: "A Story, An Encounter, and A Place Among the Ancestors."

✳   At the age of twenty-eight during my third year of seminary training, I fulfilled a dream within a dream. Not only did I travel to Africa, but I had an experience there that I had only glimpsed before in the writings of sociologists and anthropologists. These fortunate explorers described personal odysseys deep into the most remote places in the world where they met an elderly woman or a tribesman who was able to tell them the stories and history of their people. Never did it occur to me that one day I would have the same opportunity with so little effort on my part.

During the course of a two-month stay at the Lukulu mission run by the Oblates of Mary Immaculate, the Christian Brothers and the Sisters of the Holy Cross, there were many days when I would accompany one of the missionaries on long walks along the Zambezi River to visit parishioners in nearby settlements. On one occasion in early June, as a Zambian sister of the Holy Cross named Teresa and I were ambling back to Lukulu from a nearby village, Mulongo, I spotted a lone hut far away on a hillside and I asked Sr. Teresa if she knew who lived there.

"The Princess Mukwae Katauka lives there," she explained. "She's the oldest surviving member of the Lozi royal family. She lives alone because the people in Mulongo are afraid of her. They say that she has lived so long because she is a witch. I take her food once in a while. She's a great storyteller."

At the word "storyteller," I jumped. "Please take me to visit her the next time you go!" I pleaded. Sr. Teresa agreed, saying she would interpret for me.

It was one whole month before we were able to return, and I was ready with questions. On July 5, early on a bright, warm morning, Sr. Teresa and I stood knocking at Princess Mukwae's door, bearing gifts: tomatoes, peanuts, and a bag of her favorite snuff powder.

"*Odi sha! Odi sha!*" Teresa repeated the Silozi phrase for "Excuse us." Eventually, a voice answered back, sounding rather cranky and groggy. The door remained shut, and for a moment my heart sank. I was sure we were not going to be granted an audience. Sr. Teresa had warned me that the princess was a very free-spirited and independent person, who, on a bad day, might chase away even friendly visitors. After much questioning and answering through the closed door, Sr. Teresa turned to me and smiled, "She's coming out. Get ready." So we pulled up a couple of tree-stump stools and we waited.

Shortly, the ancient princess emerged from her rickety hut, dragging a sitting mat behind her. She was an impressive sight. She was bent double at the waist and had brilliant yellow eyes and teeth and wispy silver hair. Her skin was like corrugated leather stretched tight over knotted joints and bones. Yet there was something about her, a certain freedom, strength and dignity. Even though she must have dressed hurriedly and in the dark, her blue and white *chitengi* was spotless and exactly fitted around her unusual form. She did not even look at us as she spread out her mat and lowered herself onto it in a semi-recumbent position. She eyed us for a long time and then cackled with glee when Teresa produced the bag of snuff. The princess snorted some, sneezed, and then settled herself.

Teresa waited for her to speak and whenever she spoke she would address Teresa, looking at me only when I was speaking. Teresa had a notebook and pencil ready and explained several times that I wished to ask questions and hear stories. This seemed to puzzle the princess. She thought it over, took some more snuff, and sneezed again. Teresa told me that no *makua* (white man) had ever asked her to do this before. As I watched the princess, I realized that she possessed a delightful and natural self-confidence and she had a marvelous lack of self-consciousness. She seemed to take as much pleasure in sneezing as she took in the snuff itself.

The rest of that day we sat there engrossed in conversation. Once in a while Sr. Teresa would put down her pencil and stretch her neck and shoulders, gazing at the far-off Zambezi River. Then Princess Mukwae would close her eyes and start humming to herself, something between chanting and groaning. I just watched.

At one point, the princess and Teresa were going back and forth and I asked what the problem was. Sr. Teresa explained to me that it was very difficult to translate some of the expressions the princess was using because she spoke in a special, archaic dialect reserved exclusively to the members of the Lozi royal family. I was deeply grateful for Teresa's mediation and I realized that this must have been tiring for her.

Princess Mukwae never flagged. She was delighted to tell her stories and she punctuated her phrases several times with a long, bony finger that poked a design in the sand or jabbed at the sky. She used the names "Nyambe" and "Nasilele" repeatedly, and Teresa told me that these were the names of God.

In the course of our time together, I asked many questions. What could she tell me about God? How did her people pray and worship? How did the world begin? Where did her people come from? How did her family become royalty? What was her earliest memory? What magic was hidden in the waters of the Zambezi and what would the river tell me if it could speak? Why were the rain trees sacred to the Lozi? Where did the ancestors gather? When she talked with God or with the ancestors, what did they tell her? What was it like to live alone, outside Mulongo? How did her people bless and curse and heal one another? What stories had her mother and father and grandparents told her when she was a child? What was her happiest memory? What did she dream about? It would take Sr. Teresa one whole week to put all her hastily scribbled notes into a legible form for me.

Toward the end of the afternoon, I noticed that a dramatic change had suddenly come over Princess Mukwae. She seemed terribly sad. I asked why. Sr. Teresa had a long dialogue with her in a softer tone of voice and then explained to me that the great sorrow of the princess's life was that she had no children of her own and that therefore, when she died, her spirit would "diminish." The Lozi belief is that it is only through one's children that one is guaranteed a place among the ancestors. I felt a lump in my throat as I watched the weight of this sadness oppress the old woman. I had to do something about this. I had already been wondering how I could ever express my gratitude to her for this conversation.

"Tell her," I instructed Teresa slowly and deliberately, "tell her that in my land far away, my people believe that if you tell the story of a person, then that person lives on through the telling of the story. Tell her that when I return to my people far away, I will tell them of her and through this she will be remembered and her spirit will live on."

When Teresa translated this, the princess became wide-eyed and asked her to repeat it. She began to cry. I began to cry. Sr. Teresa swayed to and fro on her stool. Then the princess replied:

"Tell him that when he does this for me, I will become his ancestor. My spirit will be with him no matter how far away he goes, and he will be my son." At that point, even Teresa cried.

Soon after this, Princess Mukwae moved to get up. Sr. Teresa motioned to me to wait in silence. The princess disappeared back into her hut and closed the door. "Is it over now?" I wondered to myself. This seemed too abrupt an ending to the conversation we had just been having. Soon, however, she appeared again and beckoned me to come inside. So I did. She took great joy in pointing out to me all the contents of her little hut, every blanket, bottle and stone. I had barely noticed that Sr. Teresa had gasped when I stepped inside.

Our parting was long and needed to be repeated several times before we could leave. Finally, Princess Mukwae kissed my hand and spat into my palm. I bowed profoundly to her, stammering a blessing in my fractured Silozi. I noticed that something had come over Sr. Teresa. Only after we had walked some distance down the sandy path in silence did she stop and lean against a tree, seeming to catch her breath.

"Do you realize, do you realize what just happened?" she asked me at last.

"No. Tell me," I replied, almost holding my breath.

"I think," Teresa said thoughtfully, "you are the first white man ever to be allowed into the household of a royal family member. It is strictly forbidden for anyone but family to enter. I am a Zambian and I have been visiting her for years but not even I have ever been inside. And she gave you the special blessing with her spittle. This means you are her family now."

Princess Mukwae Katauka had given me her story. In return, I gave her my word. In telling and re-telling this encounter, I marvel at the way an ancient princess's hope and a young man's wonder brought two very different worlds together, to be sustained by a story, perhaps forever.

May our ancestors bless and be with you who read this now. May you also sustain hope and wonder in the telling of your own story.

There is ritual parting among storytellers that goes: "If there is no one to listen, is there any story to tell? I thank you for your attention to the words, for listening and taking the story to heart." All of these stories, those from ancient religious traditions and those newly crafted and added to the history by me and Tony Cowan seek to connect us to all the rest of the world, to truth-telling and, lastly, to give us a place among our ancestors, those who have gone before us in faith and have lived, passing on to us their spirit. May we give away much so that our spirits will live on undiminished in our children and our children's children to at least the fifth generation, giving great heart to this fragile world. May it be so. In the tradition of the tellers, we bow deeply before you who take our words to heart.

1

A Word about Words and Sounds

———— ✳ ————

Even your silence holds a sort of prayer. (Apache)

Earth with her thousand voices praises God.
(Samuel Taylor Coleridge)

There is an ancient story that keeps reappearing in each
age:

✳ Once upon a time it was that Tibetan monks spent their
   entire lives chanting the names of the Holy One, God.
   They believed that, when they had finished the chanting
   and the naming, all would be said and done. It would be
   finished and earth would have reached its end time. For
   time begins with God's voice, God's words, and so time
   will end with our sounding, chanting the names of the
   Holy, the unspeakable: God.
     Two men, visitors to the ancient roof of the world
   high in the Himalayas, had heard of this theory and
   stopped a monk on his journey to inquire about this idea.
   They stood in the wind, prayer flags snapping in the stiff
   breeze, and asked him if this was actually what monks
   believed and did. He looked at them intently and in the
   silence they could hear the chanting, droning coming
   from the monastery walls. He didn't answer immediately

9

and so, while waiting for his response, they began a discussion of the theory. Soon they were laughing at the idea, even with a hint of contempt for the very thought of it. But the chanting continued in the background and, as they spoke, the earth began to disappear, to be erased: grains of sand, soil, leaves, rocks, animals, birds, the prayer flags shredded and torn, even the clothing on the men as they spoke. The air thinned out even more, the sky emptied, the world turned in upon itself, and the shining eyes of the monk spoke softly: it is happening even now. We are reaching the end of the names, of what can be said.

It is said by old ones in every generation that the names of God are like the names of the stars. All words, all sounds spun from small atoms, from the alphabets of imagination, whether stuttering or magnificent, are expressions of the Creator. Each one is a fragile, tiny incarnation—an a-ha. The scientists claim we are made of stardust, nondescript dust mites, but together saying something spectacular and meaningful. And of course, we are not just talking about stars, or sounds, or even just about us. We are talking about the Holy, about communions and correspondences, about the universe. The ancient Hindu Scriptures (Vedas) of India tell of the generation of the material universe out of the "full void," an emptiness of infinite intelligence that makes everything out of silences and sounds, the fundamental energetic vibrations of divine thought. Only in recent years has Western science begun to catch up to this fundamental metaphysics of creation through the advances of quantum physics and mind-body medicine.

The stars are in motion. They are moveable feasts—like words, like notes in music, like us. We are all of a piece, one piece of the uni-verse, one unending piece of poetry, rhyme, rhythm and heart beat. Whether we are made of stardust and the music of the spheres or of skins stretched across frames to make drums or of quivering flesh and blood and bone, we are singing. Whether our words stick in our throats or move into our stomachs like butterflies, we are about saying something, expressing ourselves and connecting with others.

Even before there are words, sounds and silences already tell stories. Those stories lurk in everything: the creak of a rocking chair, footsteps on stairs, the breathing of our sisters or brothers in the same bed, snow falling, the gasps and moans of a fever of 105, whispers between parents, the crack of a bat and a ball thudding into a glove, the land being dug for a tree planting, the amaryllis sitting in the closet waiting to rebloom, the refusals to speak or looks that "could stop a clock." They are endless: the owl's cry before swift descent, the grasp and the kill and the mouse's pounding heart throbbing in fear before the claws close around its body. Or a comet visible for weeks as it moves—eventually out of range into the vast silence of the universe. If we were out "there" we would be dumb, mute, speechless, without words.

When I was young I was fascinated by stars. I would lay in the grass as it grew wet and damp and watch them come out. Pinpricks, tiny eyeholes where perhaps others and/or angels peered through at us here below. The first time I stood on a chair and telephone book and looked through a keyhole in the double-bolted door I was sure that was what it was like from the other side of night. I was sure there was another space-place out there beyond the stars. I longed to look back or to see earth the way it might look from there. When I first saw El Greco's pictures with their slanted perspectives and elongated objects I wondered, did he hear sound like that—stretched out, tensing the silence? For eyes are connected to ears, seeing to hearing, looking to listening.

What do our silences sound like? What are the colors of our sounds? And the sound of my own voice? Angels sing; do they hear? Do the tremors that show in our voices and so subtly reveal us to others entertain God? Some *koans* (loaded questions, usually encapsulated in one line) to play with: What is the sound of one hand clapping? What is the sound of a soul praying in agony? What is the sound of a heart beating? What is the sound of one person contemplating sin? What is the sound of evil looming? What is the sound of hope erased? What is the sound of a child born dead? What is the sound of waking in a tomb and being summoned to resurrection and home, at last? The first sound, the sound of God creating, does it still echo in the universe and has it seeped into every stone, tree root and piece of skin?

This isn't as strange or even as imaginative as it may seem. There is an ancient tradition among the Jews that when YHWH (certain words you do not speak aloud or even write down) spoke and gave the law on Mt. Sinai, the words were heard not just by all who were present; the words have echoed down through the ages and every human being can hear them. In fact, it's impossible not to hear them.

We have our stories in the Christian tradition that are filled with underlying sounds, past words. Lazarus was in the tomb (John 11) and Jesus cried out, summoning him forth from death, from the tomb. That voice, the Word made flesh, commands even flesh that has been rotting in a tomb for four days to surge forth, fresh, with bones knit together. What did that voice sound like? Did Lazarus ever hear anything the same way again? Or we are told that John, the child of Elizabeth and Zachary, leapt in his mother's womb and danced for joy at the sound of Mary's voice already laced with the Word made flesh (Luke 1). Did John spend all his life waiting for that voice again? This God is behind all our words. We pray repeatedly, borrowing another's words: "O Lord, I am not worthy, only say the word and I shall be healed" (sprung from the story of a man seeking healing for his son). And the holy ones of our traditions tell us that in the presence of the Holy it is we who are sounded, like tuning forks, and read, entered and sung through to glory or to endless mourning.

All stories are made of words. It is surprising how many creation stories from far-flung civilizations and geographies share a fascination with words, sounds and breath as the beginning, as that from which air, light and water have sprung, as though all were the same "stuff" rearranged in different patterns. Emily Dickinson even describes the resurrection as "a strange slant of light." And "in the beginning," even according to the astronomers, was a time of light. There are about one hundred atomic elements, the "stuff" of the universe. We have twenty-six letters in our alphabet as the "stuff" that we work with and a score of sounds to accompany our matter. The mix of matter and spirit seems to issue forth in sounds and words.

The universe is expanding, we are told. In religious or theological terms, God, the maker and keeper of all creation, breathes, sighs, expands. Everything, it seems, swells like a child in a womb. And all these words are about one thing: revelation—the uncovering and unveiling of what's already there. When we talk about stars we say they shed mass (they die). The sun has a solar wind (it breathes) and stars burn out and give birth. Matter is indestructible, though never at a standstill.

A Jewish rabbi once said: God is always revealing himself to the soul, but, like sunrises and sunsets, he never repeats. Stars fall or become shooting stars and we treasure the story of the star that rose in the east to herald the birth of the newborn king of peace, the star that led astrologers on a journey to wisdom. We count stars and live with our heads in the sky (like Galileo). And yet scientists tell us that we know only about 3 percent of the stuff in the universe! That other 97 percent—ahhhhh. And storytellers, beginning with my Nana, tell me that stars don't really fall or go shooting across the sky at random: they decide! They choose death so that someone on earth can choose life and goodness and they hurl themselves across the sky, throwing their soul and life away, siding with the weak so that they may live. In scientific terms they cast off matter.

It is all about revelation, whether we are peering through telescopes and counting stars or being accosted by burning bushes on holy ground. It is we who cannot stand the intensity of such burning light, such purity. Scientifically it is hydrogen, carbon and oxygen, but the spirit hovering, moving and stirring with something like the wings of a dove or tongues of fire, reminds us that we too are the stars of the universe, made of old molecules of stardust, and we return, we live, and pass it on somewhere. Words, matter and spirit, we ourselves exist to take the veils away from what is.

We are told:

> In the beginning, when God began to create the heavens and the earth, the earth had no form and was void; darkness was over the deep and the Spirit of God hovered over the waters.

God said, "Let there be light"; and there was
light. God saw that the light was good and he separated the light from the darkness. God called the light
'Day' and the darkness 'Night.' There was evening
and there was morning: the first day. (Genesis 1:1-5)

Five lines and the universe is set in motion. (Notice: God
began to create, so it must still be happening!) But in these
few lines and equally few words there is light, history, the beginning of time, geography, naming, separation, and goodness. There is form and something now in the void. It is all
beginning.

Much later in the Old Testament, in the book of Job (chapter 38) this God has a few more words to say about creation
and the work it takes to begin and to continue the work. In
fact Yahweh speaks about creating for four whole chapters!

Where were you when I founded the earth?
Answer, and show me your knowledge.
Do you know who determined its size,
who stretched out its measuring line?
On what were its bases set?
Who laid its cornerstone,
while the morning stars sang together
and the sons of God shouted for joy? (Job 38:4-7)

Can you bind the chains of the Pleiades,
or loosen the bonds of Orion?
Can you guide the morning star in its season,
or lead the Bear with its train?
Do you know the laws of the heavens,
and can you establish their rule on earth?
(Job 38:31-33)

Now the story of creation, in the form of questions, expresses
deeper realities—those of relationships and attitudes, of distance and unknowing, of mystery. The creation itself reveals
that there is an Other separate from creation yet bound to it

intimately, and that there is meaning to the existence of the universe and what dwells in it. After being questioned, Job answers:

> I know that you are all powerful;
> no plan of yours can be thwarted.
> I spoke of things I did not understand,
> too wonderful for me to know.
> My ears had heard of you,
> but now my eyes have seen you.
> Therefore I retract all I have said,
> and in dust and ashes I repent. (Job 42:2-6)

And yet after interrogating Job and telling him to reconsider his words, it is God who turns to Job's friends and announces that it is Job who has spoken of him rightly. Yahweh calls Job his servant and tells them that he will accept Job's prayer for them (Job 42:7-9). And Job is just, careful of all in his care, treating the poor, the orphan and the widow, the stranger, the sick and the injured with tenderness and concern. He has treated the sojourner, the wayfarer, and even his enemies with equal dignity. And he is thankful and aware of his land and crops and their relatedness to his life and family (Job 31). All of creation, of life, of history is of a piece. The story evolves and deepens and there are many versions of it (see Job's friends' versions in the many chapters prior to Job's long cry to God to answer him). We are all telling the story, using our words to shuffle our experiences and knowledge and put them in a form that we distill and accept. The story is always being retold, reinterpreted and recast, but it is the same story.

Our tradition will grow out of this story that culminates in John 1:

> In the beginning was the Word
> And the Word was with God
> and the Word was God;
> he was in the beginning with God.

All things were made through him
and without him nothing came to be.
Whatever has come to be, found life in him,
life which for humans was also light.
Light that shines in the dark:
light that darkness could not overcome. (John 1:1-5)

Another five verses! While echoing the original version of
the story, this story is inside, underneath, seeping through
and radically altering the earlier story of creation. The word
that God originally spoke to bring form to the world was, believe it or not, the Word that would become flesh and would
"pitch his tent among us." This Word was coming from the
Father and was the "fullness of truth and loving-kindness"
(John 1:14). This story says more, and—some would say—
says it better and alters our understanding of the first one.
Now we go back and hear and read the original with hind-
sight, understanding, insight, awe and wonder at what else
we might have missed! What else is hidden in there?

Every tradition, every people seeks to tell the story, to say
it their way, to give it a new twist, a turn based on their place
in the universe, their time, and their ways of expressing their
relationship to the Maker and Keeper of all things.

Ken Feit, an itinerant fool and clown who first introduced
me to stories through the meandering way of mime, clowning
and puppets, told an old Native American creation story from
the Plains tradition. As I remember it:

❋   Once upon a time when the earth was young, Coyote was
out walking. It was night and dark. Coyote ran into his
friends, the wolves. It was a company of five wolves, all
brothers, and they often shared their hunt and kill with
Coyote. This night they were all gathered together, looking
up at the dark night sky. Coyote greeted them and turned
to the sky too. But it was empty; there was absolutely
nothing there. He peered and strained his eyes to see what
they were looking at, but there wasn't anything there.

    "What are you looking at, my brothers?" And the first
one, the eldest, wouldn't say. Coyote went away.

The next night he met them again and found them gazing into the dark above them. Again he arched his head and looked, finding nothing there. "What are you looking at, my brothers?" And none of the wolves answered him. Coyote went away. This went on for nights and Coyote became disgruntled with his friends the wolves.

Finally the wolves gathered together and said, "We have to tell Coyote what we're looking at, what we've found up there. After all, what can he do? It's so far away, unreachable." And so they decided to include him in the sighting.

The next night Coyote came and found his friends gazing at the night. He asked again, "What are you looking at, my brothers?" And this time the youngest said, "Coyote, we see two large animals up there. But we don't know what they are. It's too dark and too far away."

And it was Coyote who surprised them then. "Let's go see them and get up closer."

"How?" they asked.

"Easy," said Coyote. "Watch me!" And Coyote took his bow and arrow and started shooting into the sky, arrow after arrow straight up. The first one stuck and the second latched onto that one; the third hooked onto that and so on, until there was a path, a ladder into the night. "Now," said Coyote, "let's climb." And up he went, followed by the five brothers. The oldest wolf had a dog and took him with him. They climbed and climbed all night, all day, all night, all day. It was a long journey.

Finally they drew near the animals. They were two bears! The wolves approached cautiously, all except for the oldest wolf with his dog, who watched more carefully from a distance, with Coyote. He knew that Coyote didn't trust bears and wouldn't come any closer. The wolves looked at the bears and the bears stayed still and looked back! They sat and looked at each other for a long time.

Then the old wolf began to inch away from Coyote and toward his brothers. "Don't go," whispered Coyote, "the bears will scratch and fight you; you know how fast and dangerous grizzlies are." But the old wolf continued to move ahead slowly and soon he and his dog quietly joined his brothers. They sat together, still, as though it was meant to be.

But Coyote wouldn't move any closer. He knew bears. He had had some nasty close escapes and had learned his lesson. He sat awhile, watching his friends watch the bears. "It's a nice picture," he thought to himself. "I think I'll go now, and leave them there for others to see. And when others look into the sky, they'll say, 'Ah, I bet there's a story about those bears and wolves,' and then they'll tell the story about me and my ladder to the sky. Yes, I'll leave them here."

So Coyote went back down the ladder, retrieving his arrows as he descended. Once back on the ground, Coyote turned around and looked at the arrangement of his friends in the night sky. They were still there, right where he left them. Today they're called the Big Dipper: three of the wolves are the handle and the one in the middle, the old wolf, has his dog still close by his side. The two young ones form the bow under the handle and the two grizzly bears are the other side of the bow, the side that points to the North Star.

Every night Coyote would go back and admire the picture and then he decided they might be lonely up there. Time to make more pictures, more arrangements and so, of course, there'd be more stories to tell about him! Every night for years that's what Coyote did: make pictures in the sky for others to look up at. Sometimes he got lazy, or playful, or creative and just threw his arrows up to see how far he could throw or how things would come down at random. He always had lots of ideas. Finally he made the Big Sky Road and spread it out, using up a lot of his leftover stars and arrows. Finally, he sat one night and did nothing. It was good. Night after night he just sat quietly gazing into the dark that shone and pulsed and teemed with life now. Yes, it was good!

Later on, Coyote would tell his other friends—owl, eagle, raccoon and rabbit—about his night work. And always, he'd end with the same request. "Now remember, brother or sister, who it was that arranged the stars and made the night so bright. Whenever you see anyone watching my pictures, you be sure to tell them the stories I told you, and especially, be sure to tell them that I made that story and it was I who did that in the sky. That was my night work."

And so, today, still there are animals and birds, even two-leggeds that tell this story. They heard it from their brothers and sisters who are still friends of Coyote.

It seems that work, creation, pictures, communication, stories and time are still all woven together, but they're meant to be shared. The Jewish mystical tradition says that "in the beginning" there was only the Holy One. God filled up everything, even the void. There was no place or time where God was not. There was only his radiant light and glory. But God was aware that he was the Only and, for reasons that only God knows, he desired to make something other—something like, but unlike, of, but not only of, God. So he made room inside and hollowed out a place where there would be room for the universe. He contracted and then spoke and there was light in the space, spreading out. But there was no limit or boundary and the place couldn't hold together. There was chaos. So again, God said: let there be light, attenuated light in this space. And there was. And the light moved into forms, bounded by limits. Soon there were all forms of light: angels, chariots, fiery holy beings. There was movement and the sound of movement: stars, planets, holes and galaxies, storms, winds, thunder and lightning, rain and pools of water. The light just spread and spun out into more and more attenuated beings. Last, the Holy One carefully formed human beings, men and women of every kind, and sent them to play, to explore this place and continue his making. He gave them a sense of light, of radiant glory and presence that belonged to God alone and they knew they were to concentrate on and look for that light everywhere. It was that light that they could touch and sense and grasp. It was that light that they would form and fashion into something of the Holy themselves. They could all know the Holy and direct that radiance elsewhere. And then God rested and looked at all that had been made, formed, and bounded. And it was all good and it was the beginning of time: the first Sabbath.

This is the essential teaching of Rabbi Levi Yitzhak of Berditchev, the teaching that in the beginning God had to make room for the universe and for us inside God; and that he had to try it again to get it to hold together; that it's shared, handed over as part of the essence of being human: to continue to make room for others, for all things inside God. It is give and take between God and humans and all else is included, gathered within. There is nothing else. That is the only story. All else is extra, or to be woven into the story. The way we tell the story is the uni-verse and the story is in motion, becoming. In the telling we make it, expand it, and make room for it.

This Jewish tradition is treasured and honored in every generation. Years after the death of the Baal Shem Tov (the Master of the Good Name) the Kobriner rabbi asked the Slonimer rabbi, one of that generation's great Hasidim: "Have your teachers left behind any writings as a heritage?"

"Oh yes."

"Are they printed, or are they still in manuscript form?"

"Neither," responded the Slonimer rabbi. "They are inscribed in the hearts of their disciples."

The stories, the knowledge and experiences, the wisdom and understanding live on in stories and in words, inside those who heard. The disciples cling to the presence of their teachers (*zaddik*) by speaking, by telling the stories, by acting them out, praying them, living their truth. They listened, they breathed in his spirit. Now that spirit remains in their ears and hearts and comes out of their mouths. This is more than communication; it is communion. Its reality is wordless, beyond speech or concept. There is a union, an old unity.

It is said that when he was in Calcutta in 1967, Thomas Merton remarked to an Asian monk, "We are all one already! But we forget. We imagine that we are not. What we have to recover is our original unity. What we have to be is what we already are." Thomas Merton spoke these words shortly before he died, touched by a ray of light!

"In the beginning..." always reveals what was, what could be, what the future is, what we are already. A couple of thousand years ago Marcus Aurelius, an old Roman general, sat in his tent one night and wrote in his journal:

> Always think of the universe as one living organism, with a single substance and a single soul; and observe how all things are submitted to the single perceptivity of this one whole, all are moved by its single impulse, and all play their part in the causation of every event that happens. Remark the intricacy... the complexity...

Humans have noticed and seen the unity over generations and ages of time. Aztecs have a saying, "The frog does not drink up the pond in which it lives." In Cuba, "When God gives the light of day, it is given for all."

The following story is a new story, very young still, but it sounds true. It sounds old. It was part of a sermon written for the Feast of the Ascension by Tony Cowan, based on the words of an angel to humans in Acts 1:11: "Men of Galilee, why do you stand gazing up into the heavens?"

* Once upon a time, long, long ago, there was a young woman who longed to see God. Her name was Stella. Stella was a simple girl who prayed and prayed and worked very hard, helping others all the time, but she reached the age of sixteen still not satisfied that she had seen God. So one day, she went to visit a wise old man who lived all alone out on the prairie. She sat down in front of the wise old man and said, "For as long as I can remember, I've had a burning desire to see God: not only to see God, but to look right into the pupil of his eye! If I could just do this, I would be so happy. Can you tell me what I need to do so that this can happen?"

The wise old man looked at Stella intensely. After a long silence, he said: "I will tell you the secret of seeing God—in fact, of looking right into the pupil of God's eye."

"Oh, yes! Please tell me!" the young woman cried. The old man continued: "You must begin counting the stars at night. You must begin with the middle star in Orion's belt and start counting toward the east. You must take great care not to count any star twice, and you must not fail in your determination. When you have counted the ten thousandth star, you will be looking into the very light of God's eye."

And so, Stella went out. That night, there was a new moon and there were very few clouds, so she was able to count the stars easily. They looked to Stella like diamonds embedded in velvet. After several hours, she had counted hundreds of stars. But the next night, when she went out to continue her counting, there were some heavy clouds and the moon was brighter, which made it harder for her to see the stars clearly. Still she continued resolutely, night after night, week after week, month after month, always taking care to keep count and not get distracted. This took tremendous concentration, dedication, and effort.

What Stella didn't realize was that as she counted far into the eastern sky, the stars were revolving and turning through the heavens. And so, twelve months later, as she was approaching the ten thousandth star, she began to get the feeling that the pattern in the sky looked strangely familiar. She counted aloud to herself, "Nine thousand nine hundred and ninety-eight. Nine thousand nine hundred and ninety-nine." And as she counted the ten thousandth star, she suddenly realized that the ten thousandth star was the middle star in Orion's belt, the very star she had begun with twelve months before! Her eyes were dazzled with starlight and her mind and heart were filled instantly with the greatest joy and astonishment. Time seemed to stand still as she stood rapt in wonder, gazing at the ten thousandth star, and the star seemed to be gazing back at Stella with equal intensity.

Hours later, she ran through the night across the prairie to the house of the ancient wise man. She found him awake, praying for her, and when he invited her to come in, they sat facing each other over a low table covered with lighted candles.

"Judging from your radiant smile," said the old man, "you've counted the ten thousandth star tonight, and you have looked into the very eye of God. Yes?"

"Yes! Yes!" cried Stella, scarcely able to contain her happiness. "But," she continued, "the strangest thing happened. It turned out that the ten thousandth star was somehow the very same star I had begun with, the middle star in Orion's belt. What can this mean?"

The old man smiled with delight. "It's simple," he murmured. "You began by looking into the light of God's eyes, desperately desiring to see the light of God's eye. God was there all along. You just didn't realize it. The whole sky had to move through one complete revolution just so you could recognize what was right in front of you to start with! God moved heaven and earth to bring you to this moment. That's how much God loves you! And I'll tell you something else: from now on, whenever children such as you gaze at the night sky with burning desire born of great love and wonder and purity, God will wink at them and they will catch a glimpse of the twinkle in God's eyes."

The wise old man fell silent, and Stella looked closely at the lines on his face. As a sense of wonder and love welled up inside her once again, she noticed that even now there was a twinkle in the old man's eyes!

Many many years later, another wise old man, Meister Eckhardt, would say: "The eye with which you look at God is the very same eye with which God is looking at you." Who knows?—perhaps he too had been counting the stars.

What are you doing tonight? Let us begin to count stars, name stars and recover the light in each other's eyes. The stars beckon, reveal, speak wordlessly.

Resources

Books to help you see, dream, and tell stories:
Michael J. Caduto and Joseph Bruchac, *Keepers of the Night: Native American Stories and Nocturnal Activities for Children*

(Golden, CO: Fulcrum Publications, 1994). Also in the same series, *Keepers of the Earth* (1988).

David Adams Leeming with Margaret Adams Leeming, *Encyclopedia of Creation Myths* (Santa Barbara, CA: ABC-CLIO, 1994).

Czeslaw Milosz, ed., *A Book of Luminous Things: An International Anthology of Poetry* (New York: Harcourt, Brace, 1996).

Jean Guard Monroe and Ray A. Williamson, *They Dance in the Sky: Native American Star Myths* (Boston: Houghton Mifflin, 1987).

Jerrie Oughton, *How the Stars Fell into the Sky: A Navajo Legend* (Boston: Houghton Mifflin, 1992).

Chet Raymo, *The Soul of the Night: An Astronomical Pilgrimage* (Englewood Cliffs, NJ: Prentice Hall, 1985). See also Raymo's *365 Starry Nights*.

Victor Villasenor, *Walking Stars: Stories of Magic and Power* (Houston: Pinata Books, 1994).

Song Nan Zhang, *Five Heavenly Emperors: Chinese Myths of Creation* (Plattsburg, NY: Tundra Books, 1994).

Avivah Gottlieb Zornberg, *The Beginning of Desire: Reflections on Genesis* (New York: Image Books, Doubleday, 1995).

2

Opening Your Mouth

Utterance and the Unspeakable

———— ✳ ————

No more words. Hear only the voice within.
(Rumi)

The rhythm of my own heart is the birth and
death of all that are alive. (Thich Nhat Hanh)

✳ Once upon a time, when the earth was still covered by
great forests, there lived in an ancient wood a simple
woodcutter. He had lived there all his life, like his father
and grandfathers before him, marking trees for the
axman. He was good at his living, being careful to search
out the split trees, those struck by lightning, or rotting
from disease, or just broken from old age. If birds had
nested in an old pine or a family of squirrels or woodmice
had chosen a sagging tree for a comfortable home, he
silently crossed these trees off his list. They no longer belonged to the woodcutter, but to the forest.

For years he had lived this way, every day, marking
out the trees. Every day, that is, but one. One day each
year he singled out the best tree in the forest and sacri-
ficed it. From the very heart of the tree, he took the finest
wood and made a musical instrument. Each year he made

just one, and a different one each year. He had been doing it now for over a decade, in the tradition of his family. And all year long, he took the instrument with him into the woods at evening to play and to make music for the forest trees and creatures to hear—since they had given the best of their own in order to make the gift. He had fashioned a cello (named Hilary), a flute, an oboe, a piano, an organ, a violin—all the woodwinds. Each was more precise and purer in tone than the one he had made before.

This year, though, he just couldn't seem to find the right tree. He spent many hours looking for the tree. And, as the day approached, he grew sad. No tree would give up its heart, the heart he needed to make the music this year.

On the very eve of the great day, as he walked through the still woods, seeing the night falling softly and the sky turning slate blue, he was ready to admit that there would be no new music this year. And then—just as he was about to go home to sleep—he saw the tree, standing in the waning light, shadowing the ground. He couldn't understand it. Why hadn't he noticed it before? He walked up close to the tree and in the gathering darkness he could barely make out the outline of the young girl who slept, curled up against the trunk of the tree.

She looked so peaceful that he didn't want to wake her up, so he crossed over and sat down under an oak opposite her to wait. Time passed and he slept. Then, as the night sounds grew louder, he awoke to find her wide-eyed and watching him intently. She didn't seem surprised to see him, and it was almost as if she had been the one waiting for him, rather than the other way around. It was she who spoke first.

"I am the spirit of the wood. I have come to put a question to you, and you have until morning to give me an answer. Every year you have taken the heart of my best trees to make your music. Who are you to do such a thing? Why do you take them? What price are you willing to pay for your music and our hearts?"

Stunned, the woodsman was silent. After a while, he got up and went off to walk in his woods again, so unsure now, so troubled at the wood spirit's questioning.

All night he walked, sometimes weeping, pondering her words. "Why?" Why had he taken the wood? He had always thought it belonged to him. He had been careful to return the music to the forest and to go each evening to play for the trees.

As the light began to slide its winding way through the lines of trees, he still had no answer for the girl. His heart was raw—like the open wound a saw might make in the trunk of a tree. He understood the girl's question but still had no answer for her. All he had was his own suffering, his longing for his music in the forest, and his tears for all the trees of the past—the ones given for music and the ones that went for fires to provide warmth, or for homes to provide shelter from the night and storms.

She stood waiting for him by the tree, which was more magnificent in the sunlight than it had been in the shadows. And he spoke finally, stuttering over the words: "I took as a gift to give as a gift. I have nothing as repayment."

"Yes, you do," she spoke, almost laughing. "Your heart—it does make the most precious music, you know." And then, smiling, she handed him his ax.

As he cut the tree down he sang, knowing that his heart was no longer his, but all the wood of the forest was his, and there was music enough for a lifetime of giving away. He knew, now, the reason for her questions, and the reason for his living, "that when you have nothing left to give, then perhaps you have begun to live with gracefulness." The day began gloriously, as it always does, and the music of his ax and a song of his heart rang through the woods like bells on a clear, bright September day. (Written for Paul, on his diaconate ordination, Sept. 1979)

All languages begin with sounds, utterances, tones—in a word, music. Originally stories, like prayers, were sung. The breath, the air, and the spirit were intimates. Where I live in

New Mexico, the state itself is referred to by the natives as "the land of enchantment." And within an hour of where I live there is a place called Enchanted Mesa. I climb it at least once or twice a year to hear the ones who dwell up there, high above the desert floor, tell the story of what happened to their ancestors in that place.

＊ Once all the people lived on top of the mesa. It was a good life. They were safe from their enemies below and could easily guard the few steep ways up. They relied on the winds, the Spirits, for water. They lived close to the sky and in harmony with the seasons, following the old ways, the rituals, prayers, and dances that so delighted the Spirits of the place. Because it was a good life, there were some (and as time passed more and more) people who gradually fell away from the old ways. They took for granted the goodness of rain, thunder and lightning, and water, the coming of spring and winter. They neglected to pray, to be thankful, and to acknowledge what was given as gift.

And the Great Spirit was not pleased. Warnings were given—less water, too much water, harsh winters and equally harsh summers—but few heeded the signs. One year it was worse: there were only a few old ones willing to do the dances and tell the stories and offer corn to the Great Spirit in thanksgiving for harvest and in hope of good plantings. There were not enough people to do these things with respect. That night there was a terrible storm and all the paths up to the mesa were destroyed. There was much destruction of homes and carefully preserved water. In the morning when the sun appeared, the people realized to their horror that they were trapped on top of the mesa with no way down.

The days and weeks passed. There was no rain. There was less and less food and finally no water. The people prayed. They sang. They danced, but the sky was unresponsive. It would thunder and clouds would gather and approach but no water would fall from the skies. The people cried out, pleading and moaning. In time there was only silence above, except for the sound of the Spirits singing in the night, faint echoes of a people that once was strong.

The mesa is inhabited again by families that honor the old ways and keep the steep steps up toward the sky passable. And they show visitors around their pueblo and tell the stories, emphasizing the need to remember, to sing, to pray, and to be grateful for all.

The word "enchant" means to cast a spell over, to delight, to charm greatly. It comes from the Latin, *incantare*, meaning to sing or chant magical words or sounds over, to entice within. There has always been a sense of power associated with specified verbal formulas, spoken or sung aloud, repeated, or intoned silently within. And those who could sing had power, had the presence of another—of the Spirit—within them. In the first book of Samuel we hear the story of the Spirit with David as he heals and calms Saul's tormented soul.

* Samuel then took the horn of oil and anointed him in his brothers' presence. From that day onwards, Yahweh's Spirit took hold of David. Then Samuel left for Ramah.

The spirit of Yahweh had left Saul and an evil spirit sent by Yahweh tormented him. Saul's servants said to him, "We know that an evil spirit sent by God is tormenting you. If you so wish, your servants who stand before you will look for someone who can play the lyre so when the evil spirit from God comes over you, he will play and you will feel better."

So Saul answered them, "Get someone who can play the lyre well." One of them said, "A son of Jesse, the Beth-lehemite, plays very well. He is, moreover, a courageous man, intelligent and pleasant to talk with and Yahweh is with him."

So Saul sent messengers to Jesse and asked for his son David who tended the sheep. Jesse loaded an ass with bread, a wineskin and a kid and had David take all these to Saul. David then left and entered Saul's service. Saul grew very fond of David and made him his armor-bearer.

Then he sent word to Jesse, saying, "Let David remain in my service for I am very pleased with him."

So, whenever the evil spirit from God overpowered Saul, David would play on the lyre and Saul would feel better for the evil spirit would leave him. (1 Samuel 16:13-23)

The Spirit of Yahweh is wedded to sound, to music. It is as if the Spirit has a voice in the body of another person, one chosen by God. This voice of God sounded in Moses' mind and heart but all the people of Israel heard it in the desert wilderness of Sinai. In Deuteronomy we are told the story of the children of Yahweh in the presence of God at Mount Horeb when God spoke to them:

"Gather the people before me that they may hear my words. Thus they will fear me as long as they live in that land and will teach these words to their children."

Then you came nearer and stood at the foot of the mountain. It was burning in flames reaching up to heaven amid the dense fog and the dark clouds. And Yahweh spoke to you from the midst of the fire. You heard the sound of words but did not see any figure; you only heard a voice. And Yahweh spoke to you that you might know his Covenant by which he command-ed you to keep his ten commandments, which he had written on two slabs of stone. (Deuteronomy 4:10-13)

"You heard the sound of words but did not see any figure; you only heard a voice." That voice of God remains in the world and the people of Yahweh are exhorted continuously throughout their history to listen to that voice, to attend to it and to know its sound and timbre. To listen is a command of God to the people. The God of the Israelites is close to them, and he listens whenever they call out to him (Deut 4:7). And they are reminded during their sojourn in the desert that when they enter their new land they will be tempted to wor-ship other gods, to listen to other values, and this will offend God. And God will scatter them. They are told:

There [where you are scattered] you will be obliged to serve their gods, gods made by human hands, gods of wood and stone, which do not see or hear, or eat or feel. There you will look for Yahweh, your God, and you will encounter him if you search for him with all your heart and with all your soul in the midst of your anguish. When this happens in the last days, you will return to Yahweh, and you will listen to his voice. Because Yahweh, your God, is a merciful God who will not reject you nor destroy you all, nor forget the Covenant he swore to your fathers. (Deuteronomy 4:28-31)

This voice of the Holy One reveals mercy, attentiveness, and expectation. The voice is near, waiting to be summoned, to be heard and obeyed. The Rule of St. Benedict begins with the word: *Ausculta*—listen! And St. Bernard of Clairvaux said: "If you wish to see; listen." It is said that the word *listen* can just as easily be translated as *obey*—the meanings are so close. The world of the spirit, the realm of the holy, is encountered and entered into by listening and obeying.

So, then, who are we listening to? What are we listening for? The voice of God is singular and yet it can sound through others, like Moses, or Joshua, or Miriam, or David. It can sound through the prophets who speak the voice of God entreating the people to hear, to remember and to obey again.

This voice, this Spirit of God moves; it comes and goes; it visits, stays, and leaves. Once Saul is anointed king in Israel, he possesses the Spirit of God and it possesses him, but his choices and his actions drive the Spirit from him and it goes— "it rushes" upon David, and stays with him. One of the ancient marks of the presence of the Spirit of God with a person is found in that person's ability to sing, to make music, to tell stories which not only enchant, ease, and heal but also enthrall with warning, with power, and with destructive possibility. The voice breathes life and takes it away.

This sounding, this giving voice, is critical in revelation, in expressing which god is true. There is a very familiar Midrash in the Jewish community about Abram (later Abraham) and his ability to distinguish between gods. It is said that his father Terah's trade was making idols.

* Abram and his father Terah lived in the city of Haran (in present day Turkey) and made fine clay statues. These statues were in constant demand, for people bought them and took them home to set up altars and worship them, prostrating themselves before them, invoking their blessings and protection. Young Abram helped his father in the shop and would ask questions: "Father, why do they worship lumps of clay, things that we make and that can break if dropped?" His father ignored him and told him to be quiet and work and help sell the images.

  Abram would greet the people when they came into the shop and he would ask questions of those who bought the idols. One day an old man came in and pointed out an idol he wanted to buy. Abram asked him how old he was. Startled, the man snapped, "Sixty-five." And Abram then asked, "Why are you buying an idol that is only two days old when you already are much older and wiser than what we just made?" The man left without buying and Abram was cuffed for the loss of a sale.

  Another came, a woman frantic and frightened. Her house had been broken into and she had been robbed. She wanted the biggest idol she could find for protection. Abram said, "Why don't you steal an idol? It's as easy as stealing anything else." He picked one up and brought it over to her. She too left without buying. Another cuff for a lost sale.

  One night Abram couldn't sleep. He walked in the desert, enchanted by the thousands of stars in the night sky. They calmed him. They were surer than any idol he helped his father make. He worshiped the stars, but then noticed the moon. It was stronger and brighter and he thought about worshiping the moon. But the sun soon rose over the sand and pushed back the edges of night. The power of the sun was stronger; he would worship the sun. Sometimes he thought he should worship the clouds, the rain, the wind. One day he thought, "I do not see what makes the sun to rise, or the moon to wane, or the wind to blow, although I hear it. There must be something behind all of these things that I cannot see. That is what I shall worship." After that night of insight, he crept into his father's shop and smashed all the idols.

In the morning his father was furious and asked what could have happened. Abram said, "It must have been the idols. Maybe they had a fight. Look, that big one over there has a huge hammer beside him."

As he spoke, he smiled, and his father was enraged, screaming: "Idols can't quarrel. They can't even talk!"

Abram looked at his father and agreed, adding, "Then, why worship them? They are dumb, mute, and without any power. They are certainly not gods. How can they be?"

Abram's father was silent and Abram told him of his discovery, of the One behind the stars, the moon and sun, the winds and the desert, greater than anything made, invisible but there/here nonetheless. This god was the only god that Abram and his family would ever worship. This one spoke: in winds, in thunder, in all seasons.

And when we meet Abram in Genesis 12 we are told: "Yahweh said to Abram, 'Leave your country, your family and your father's house, for the land I will show you. I will make you a great nation. I will bless you and make your name great, and you will be a blessing. I will bless those who bless you, and whoever curses you, I will curse, and in you all peoples of the earth will be blessed.' So Abram went as Yahweh had told him, and Lot went with him." (Genesis 12:1-4)

Abram learns to listen to what this God says and to obey him. Later, Abraham will be one who walks and talks with God, entertaining him and his angels, cajoling God to save a city, debating with God like a good Jewish bargainer. God's first word to Abram is "Leave"—go on a journey, expand, spread out. Abram is missioned, sent forth into the unknown, into mystery that will become a history, a religion, a relationship and a blessing for all who have ears to hear, and obey.

A closer translation to the word used, other than "leave" as it is rendered in our texts, is the Hebrew translation meaning "get yourself out of your land..." (*lekh lekha*). It is repeated, intensified, and Abram is one who worships God in his deeds, in his moving forth as well as in his intensity of attention. This is God's first command to Abram and he goes. And in the going, the stories begin; the Spirit of God goes with him and his family and continues to speak to him.

Earlier we saw that Saul had lost the Spirit of God and that it came instead to stay with David. Although Saul desired God and longed to hear the Voice, he no longer worshiped in deed and action. The Voice, the Spirit, went where it would be welcomed and obeyed. That Spirit still resides in voice, in our voices. Bernice Johnson Reagon of the gospel group Sweet Honey in the Rock speaks of hearing this voice when she listens to her students, or to an audience that she tries to get to sing with her. She speaks of a sound, a spirit in a person that is recognizable beyond the music, the control, the range, the style. She notes that older members of her church might say, "The child's got a nice voice but I don't feel nothing" (Reagon, p. 15). This "voice"—this something as opposed to nothing—is the soul of a person. In the words of Joachim-Ernst Berendt,

> In Latin the term *personare* means "to sound through something." Thus, at the base of the concept of person (the concept of that which really makes a human being an unmistakable, singular per-sonality) stands the concept of sound: "through the tone." If nothing sounds through from the bottom of the being, a human being is human biologically, at best, but is not a per-son, because he does not live through the son (the tone, the sound). He does not live the sound which is the world. (Berendt, p. 171)

Deep inside is our sound, our spirit. It is that which is uncovered and let loose when we sing, chant, or tell a story. It is not just a singular sound, and perhaps it is heard best in a community. Our history of salvation begins with God hearing that sound in his people, burdened in Egypt. When Moses approaches the burning bush he is told who is speaking to him. In response,

> Moses hid his face lest his eyes look on God. Yahweh said, "I have seen the humiliation of my people in Egypt and I hear their cry when they are cruelly treated by their taskmasters. I know their suffering. I have come down to free them from the power of the Egyptians and to bring them up from that land to a beautiful spacious land, a land flowing with milk and honey. (Exodus 3:6b-8)

God's ears, so to speak, are finely tuned to the sound of suffering that reveals the soul of his people. Their cries are heard and draw God near. So many of the psalms, songs, and prayers of the Jewish people—as well as those of Christians, Muslims, and many others—are couched in sighs, moans, weeping; they are not so much words as wailing and entreaty. In Jerusalem there is the remnant of the temple wall, named the Wailing Wall, where Jews continue their cries to God, rocking back and forth silently, or softly moaning, or singing out their need for the Holy to hear them.

And the opposite is also true: moments of intense joy, delight, and awe overflow into psalm and song: "Enter his gates with thanksgiving, his courts with praise. Give thanks to him and bless his name" (Psalm 100:4) or "I will sing of your love and justice; to you, O Lord, I will sing praise" (Psalm 101:1). The examples are endless: "Bless the Lord, my soul! Clothed in majesty and splendor; O Lord, my God, how great you are!" (Psalm 104:1). So many of the psalms are entreaties to God: "Break your silence, O God whom I praise, now that the wicked and deceitful hurl their false accusations at me" (Psalm 109:1-2), or "Hear a just cause, O Lord, listen to my complaint. Give heed to my prayer for there is no deceit on my lips" (Psalm 17:1). These songs are dialogue, back and forth, two-part harmony. And just one word can express so much: Ah—Alleluia, Amen, Hosanna—this sound *ah* is connected to the heart. Positioned before another name, especially the name of

God, it is an utterance that has layers of meaning yet is not a word. Depending on tone, accent, duration, it can signify desire, ache, sorrow, need, delight, jubilation, freedom, wonder and desolation. It is a vocabulary, a story in itself.

There is another creation story told by Hafiz, a fourteenth-century Persian poet and mystic. It is said that God made a statue of clay in his own image and then asked the soul to take up residence, to enter into the clay. But the soul wanted freedom and space and saw the clay as a prison in which to be locked away. It sought to escape, to deny the creator the request. God saw the hesitation and quickly commanded the angels to sing and make music. The sound stopped the soul from escaping and stilled it, then spun it and moved it to ecstasy. Finally, as the music made clear what God was asking, the soul slipped into the clay and the first human was born. Hafiz was said to have added, "People say the soul, on hearing that song, entered the body: but in reality the soul itself is song" (Khan, p. 71).

Singing is intrinsic to our being human, whether we are singing without thought, humming our way through the day, or singing in tandem with others. We could be playing with our voices, trying to discover what we are feeling, or straining in hard labor, as the slaves did in the fields or pulling barges up rivers, or joining with others in songs shared seasonally at Christmas, Easter and other celebrations of national or familial meaning.

In the ancient Gaelic tradition there is a battle of poetic incantation in which two persons, Amergin and Cessair, stand on opposite sides of water and sing power back and forth, battling for control of the land and its resources and people. According to legend, the poetess Cessair stood on the land at the water's edge and sought to sing off and away from Ireland the warrior poet Amergin, who sought to tame the waters and gain a foothold on Irish soil. Cessair and the Irish yielded. None of the actual words remain, but people talk of them in pubs and farmhouses and spin out what they think was said, singing what they would use to throw as words and sounds into the wind. Oh, if only all our battles were still fought in this way!

These sounds are not just in humans or four-legged creatures and birds (another story altogether) and even fish, but in the land itself. There are many places that sing. All you have to do is be silent and learn to hear the voices that slowly emerge out of the silence: Chaco Canyon Anasazi ruins, the Chapel of Chimayo in northern New Mexico, any canyon lands, the desert at night, forty-million-year-old caves in Texas, old churches, seacoasts, deep old-growth forests, ancient medieval churches, to name just a few. In fact, almost any naturally or deliberately enclosed space outdoors begins to give up its song if we are quiet. Ancient drawings on cave walls and exposed rock tell of music rising and descending.

An Eskimo shaman, Orpengalih, says: "All my being is song. I sing as I draw my breath." Lilly White Feather, Cherokee, reminds us of ancient wisdom:

> Stones are like lonely old people, standing and waiting to be sung to. Our people have always sung songs of admiration to the qualities of strength, beauty and endurance that stones bring to the world. They are tired and lonely now because the white world has become so blind and selfish. They live in a hollow unsung world. (Lawlor, p. 41)

Native Americans speak of spirit lines, spider webs of energy and power. It is said that when they first saw the globes of the world that were brought by the Portuguese and Spanish and noticed the latitude and longitude lines encircling the earth, they smiled and said they too knew about the web that was spun by the Great Spirit, or Spider Woman, that held the world together. Of course, they were not understood. Such language, such images did not fit with the more scientific explanations, though they were no less valid and descriptive, perhaps even more so.

The Australian Aborigines have become famous for their songlines, often called ley lines in Western Europe, laid down by ancient peoples or gods, songlines that link and transverse the entire earth with lines of power. The Aborigines believe these songlines literally sang the world into existence and keep it alive. They link all the tribes to the old ones, their Ancestors who walked and sang with the gods. The world was named by singing (much as Adam named the animals and birds and every living creature). The ancients walked and threw out sounds and named as they traveled the land. Such singing is a knowing, a power and an exchange, a web and connection to the past. It is continued in mythic tellings, in rituals and dancing, and in continued walking; for every place, shrub, plant, insect, indentation in the earth, piece of sky speaks knowledge that is crucial to survival and to self-identity. It acts like connective tissue to hold the community together and make it human. What is inside humans is connected to what is outside in geography and objects. Once you know the song, you can never get lost—anywhere in the world, in the universe!

This is a near universal idea. Up in the northwest coasts of Washington, Vancouver, and British Columbia, they tell of navigators who know the songs of the sea, the tides, the coves and inlets. If these men are out on the ocean and get lost in a storm, they sing the songs they sang going out in reverse so they can get back home.

All the Native American tribes that have ever shared their stories with me agree that telling their creation stories was crucial to the survival of the human race and the world as we know it. Most of these stories last 365 days and each tribe is very careful and specific regarding what pieces of the story are told on what days (or nights) and in what season (winter especially). There is no allowance for change, for the sound of the words creates again or can just as surely destroy, or uncreate. And they do not care whether others believe the way they do or think that the stories and the songs are important. They know and say: just because you do not believe in the stories and in the tellings doesn't mean we are not holding the world together!

Sounds, songs, chants, tones, notes, scales, rhythms, repetitions, mantras thrown into the air move the world and give us a way to steer through the seasons, countries, borderlines, and outer spaces. Just how strong and how intimate this sound, this song can be is revealed in this line: "I'm listening to what the pot is telling me to do. I'm just a maker" (Dextra

Quotskuyva, potter from the Tewa/Hopi nations). And in other native communities the song is publicly crucial to an individual's standing in the tribe. "To Navajos, a person's worth is determined by the stories and songs she or he knows, because it is by this knowledge that an individual is linked to the history of the entire group" (Luci Tapahonso, writer). In a tradition long removed in distance and time from the Native Americans, the Buddhist Zen Master Hakuin writes, "Both singing and dancing are voices of the Way."

In the Christian tradition, listening to the voice that gives identity and power to those who can hear is essential to our belief, to our knowing who we are and how we are to live. In Matthew's account of the transfiguration, Jesus takes Peter, James and John up the mountain, apart, to pray with him. There are two kinds of sounds in this story: empty, without true understanding, and full, brimming with revelation that demands to be contemplated and swallowed, digested and taken within to be understood.

Jesus is transfigured before them, appearing in dazzling white garments, his face shining like the sun, his appearance changed. Moses and Elijah are with him. It is Peter who speaks first, without thinking, suggesting they build something to mark the place, the time, the experience. He proposes making tents, one each for Moses, Elijah, and Jesus. And even as he speaks, he is interrupted by a voice:

> Peter was still speaking when a bright cloud covered them in its shadow, and a voice from the cloud said: "This is my Son, the Beloved, my Chosen One. Listen to him."
>
> On hearing the voice, the disciples fell to the ground, full of fear. But Jesus came, touched them and said, "Stand up, do not be afraid." When they raised their eyes, they no longer saw anyone except Jesus. And as they came down the mountain, Jesus commanded them not to tell anyone what they had just seen, until the Son of Man be raised from the dead. (Matthew 17:5-9)

The voice reveals wisdom, assigns identity, and commands: Listen to him! The voice itself evokes fear, not cringing, groveling fear but the kind of awe that calls forth awareness of what one is and what one is not. The sound itself truth-tells and re-orders creation. It is confirmation for Jesus and announcement and proclamation for the disciples. They are humbled by the sound of the voice, disoriented and brought to their knees. Jesus' touch speaks to them, providing reassurance and security, humanness that re-orders and structures life once again into the familiar. But they are commanded again by Jesus' voice not to tell anyone about what has happened, what they have heard and seen, until the Son of Man be raised from the dead, until something happens that is inconceivable but will give meaning to what has transpired on the mountaintop. They are ordered to be silent, to let the voice enter them and stay, echoing and singing repeatedly within them; to allow the Spirit to teach them meaning and depth; to be tuned according to the ways of God. And they are to do this as a way of life, by listening to Jesus, Son of God, Son of the Father, Chosen One, Beloved of God.

But, notice that they immediately talk—asking about another issue altogether. They don't want to hear, can't hear, aren't open to what has happened to them, refuse to let the sound and the words about death settle inside them. And so, they chatter theologically, avoiding the mystery and the awesomeness of what just happened to them. And what happened to them was that they were invited near, given a glimpse of God. They not only overheard the Voice of the Holy, but were spoken to directly by it.

Who are we listening to? What are we saying? What is revealed by our silences and our sounds? What are we professing as belief and staking our lives on?

We teach by words, by sounds, by music, by silences. Some of the most famous lessons, *koans* of Zen Buddhism, are found in a tome called *The Gateless Gate (Mumonkan)* supposedly composed by the Zen monk Mumon Ekai in 1228. This is case number 32 in which a non-Buddhist philosopher questions the Buddha.

❋   A philosopher asked the Buddha, "Without words, without the wordless, will you tell me truth?"

The Buddha kept silence.

The philosopher bowed and thanked the Buddha, saying, "With your loving kindness I have cleared away my delusions and entered the true path."

After the philosopher had gone, Ananda asked the Buddha what the philosopher had attained.

The Buddha replied, "A good horse runs even at the shadow of the whip."

Buddha's silence—his *samadhi*—was the subtle lesson that the master taught to the philosopher. The subtlety of the teaching is like the shadow; the impact of enlightenment is the whip. (From *Koans: The Lessons of Zen*, p. 30)

Our silences reveal; what sounds through us speaks volumes. What are we saying? What word are we uttering? Do we speak in tongues of angels, of others' mindless chatter? Or does the Voice of God find a way through us into the space of the world? If we had only one sound to make, one revelation to share, one word that would be our legacy and song, what would it be?

What follows is a psalm. Sing it aloud and see how it sounds. Then, write your own. Pick a line from scripture and start singing it softly. Play with the words, tone, notes. See where it takes you and what you hear in the words, what is given to you, what comes to you from the silence and from under the sound. Sing, chant, enchant, pray, speak, and then be silent again. Worship.

Refrain:

Saul, Saul, Why do you persecute me? It is I the Lord, who is hurt, weary of hate and crying in pain. Can you not see: these are the ones who reveal my name.

Verses:

Look to the children so hungry and cold
Begging for life and the chance to grow old.

Look to the old ones so fragile and weak
Murmuring my presence that is simple and meek.

Look to the beggars, the lost and the lame
Hoping for kindness, and a life without shame.

Look to the ones who struggle in vain
Waiting for justice and mercy to reign.

Look to the poor, the blind and the lost
Seeking for dignity, reckoning its cost.

Look to the tortured, the innocent killed
Silently demanding with their blood that is spilled.

Look to the truthteller, the singers so bold
Making sure that my story is continuously told.

Look to the ones that are non-violent and pray
Storming at heaven and preparing my way.

There are songs in everything. The universe is made of music
...and of stories looking for sound.

Resources

Books

Joachim-Ernst Berendt and Fritjof Capra, *Nada Brahma: The World Is Sound* (Rochester, Vermont: Destiny Books, 1987).
Orson Scott Card, *Songmaster* (New York: Tom Doherty, 1987).
Bruce Chatwin, *The Songlines* (New York: Penguin Books, N.Y., 1987); in particular for Aborigine beliefs and sense of space.
Kenneth Grahame, *The Wind in the Willows* (New York: Charles Scribners, 1960).
Joan Halifax, *Shamanic Voices* (New York: E. P. Dutton, 1979); on sound in primitive cultures.

Hazrat Inayat Khan, *The Music of Life* (Sante Fe: Omega Books, 1983).

Robert Lawlor, *Voices of the First Day: Awakening in the Aboriginal Dreamtime* (Rochester, Vermont: Inner Traditions, 1991).

Manuela Dunn Mascetti, ed., *Koans: The Lessons of Zen* (New York: Hyperion, 1996).

Ann McCaffrey, *Dragon Song, Dragon Singer,* and *Dragon Drums* (New York: Bantam Books, 1977, 1978, 1980).

Simon Ortiz, *Song, Poetry and Language: Expression and Perception* (Tsaile, AZ: Navajo Community College Press, 1977).

Bernice Johnson Reagon, *We Who Believe in Freedom: Sweet Honey in the Rock... Still on the Journey* (New York: Anchor Books, 1993).

David Steindl-Rast, with Sharon Lebell, *The Music of Silence: Entering the Sacred Space of Monastic Experience* (San Francisco: Harper, 1995); in particular for general concepts and changing attitudes, to help one hear better.

Two Zen Classics: The Gateless Gate and the Blue Cliff Records, trans. Katsuki Sekida (New York: Weatherhill).

Laurens Van der Post, *The Lost World of the Kalahari* (New York: Harcourt Brace Jovanovich, 1958).

Poetry

Read poetry from every culture, especially bi-lingual poetry, silently and aloud.

Music

Ancient Voices, Vox Sacra, a selection of various artists, Harmonia mundi, 1995.

Anonymous 4, *An English Ladymass, Voices of Light, The Lily and the Lamb* (medieval chants, carols and polyphony).

Dead Can Dance, *Toward the Within* (and anything by them). Hard to describe but worth listening to and finding.

Kitaro, *Oasis* (Japanese), and numerous other pieces.

Koorunba, *Walkabout,* music from cultures as diverse as India, Aboriginal Australia, Greece, and others.

Noirin Ni Riain, *River of Stars, Stor Amhran, The Virgin's Lament, Celtic Soul, Vox de Nube, Soundings, The Darkest Midnight*. She is an Irish singer with the Glenstal Abbey, Limmerick, who sings ancient Irish music, chant, Old Gaelic style, usually sung in English, Latin and Gaelic.

Shomyo: Buddhist Liturgical Chant, alternative sounds, tones.

Any kind of chant: Gregorian, Eastern Church, Russian Orthodox, Sufi, and so on.

3

Tell Me a Story

Oral and Written Traditions

———— ✳ ————

Stories are Beings. You invite them to live with you. They'll teach you what they know in return for being a good host. When they're ready to move on they'll let you know. Then you pass them on to someone else. (Cree Storyteller)

Sir Ramakrishna was asked: "Why, God being good, is there evil in the world?" He answered: "To thicken the plot."

There are teachers, preachers, wise ones, who say that everything written down is primarily a mnemonic device, a net to ensnare memory, a jumping off point for taking the story off the page. This is especially so in regard to the scriptures, not just Judeo-Christian texts, but the scriptures of all the major religions. Hillel, a famous sage of the Jewish community, once said that when one reads the Torah (the first five books of the Bible, though often the prophets and books of wisdom are also included) all one needs is respect for the text...the rest is interpretation! It is as though we are to approach a text as if it were the script for a play.

The difference between reading a play and seeing it performed is monumental. The difference between seeing a play performed and being part of the play itself, interpreting the role, is doubly monumental. Seeing a story printed on a page and then hearing it on a tape reveals enormous shifts and discoveries. Telling the story is a work that introduces the text in a unique way, filtering it through mind, heart, culture, and body. The teller incarnates the words, and those who hear the story subtly alter the presentation and delivery.

In the area of publishing there is a furious battle over who owns the story, or this particular written version of a story. Even among storytellers themselves this is an issue of contention. There is a basic split between those who believe you cannot buy and sell words that you learned from others—that stories belong to the people who have made them and told them over generations—and those who hear a story, interpret it, print it, and copyright it as their own, often without respecting the source, the ground of the insights. When you write your own story you know what you are intending to say and you can read it or tell it as you wish, but when another hears your story and tries to tell it—ah, that is another story altogether!

I have written a good ten or twelve stories of my own and a good number of them are in this book. I have never told most of them out loud (with one or two notable exceptions). I am too close to them and the effort to translate them from the written word to the spoken word is an extraordinary labor. A good many of the original stories in this book were written by my friend Tony Cowan. I tell a number of his stories, after having listened to him tell them first as well as having read them. The original writer or the teller of the tale is the finest and truest interpreter. To tell a story aloud to the writer, the crafter of the tale, is terrifying for both teller and writer. This is because, in a sense, the whole being—mind, soul, heart, and flesh—of the writer is in the words. When you tell a story you incarnate it in your own body and soul as you attempt to share it with others. The words of the story are transformed in the flesh of both writer and teller.

In telling others' stories, I try to meet with them first and then give them a private telling (not a performance). It is a ritual of asking permission, of being delegated to tell this particular story. If the story belongs to a tribe or a group of people or another religious tradition, I try to tell the story to one or a group of those who "own" the story and have them check it for truth and style and understanding. I also seek their permission to continue telling it. Their listening and discussion afterwards is the permission. Only then do I use it with other groups that would find the story new or different from their own culture and beliefs, or similar in some regards.

The stories I am most comfortable telling are those that have roots in the Judeo-Christian scriptures and culture, Buddhist stories that have marked similarities to the parable form used by Jesus, and Native American stories generally. (Coyote stories are an exception for cultural and religious reasons. Told in religious situations to relieve tensions, they evoke wild laughter [catharsis] and are strongly layered with sexual connotations and overtones of mores that are very different from those of Western civilization.) When I use a story in a text, such as this book, I will usually have told the story to a group, and often take the recorded version of the story word for word from the tape itself rather than from any written version. This offers protection regarding copyright laws, but it also is closer, truer to the way I tell the stories and to what I hope is heard, or read. And when people come to me, asking for permission to tell one of the stories they have heard me tell, I follow the same pattern. I ask them to tell me the story back as they heard it, exhorting them to use it only as it was intended and not for their own benefit. I remind them of the importance of crediting where it came from: not just me, but the sources that go farther back—the people who created the story, the culture, nation, tribe, religion from which it comes.

Sometimes I find a story in a book, or even on a scrap of paper. Then I go through the process of taking the story, the words, off the paper and putting them in my mouth. This is an art, a way of living, and a discipline. It involves constant daily practice and reaching for depth and understanding. It involves learning how to "learn it by heart" rather than memorize it, and how to honor the text itself while not being enslaved by it.

This discipline is most easily and most demandingly exercised with the scriptures, because the Word of God does not take kindly or well to being changed, altered or misused. I practice learning whole chunks of the scriptures, both the New and Earlier Testaments, and honoring the words, respecting the text itself as inspired, inspirited and incarnated this time in me. I study the text as though I were practicing to walk a tightrope without a net, because—like most storytellers and preachers and teachers in every religious tradition—I believe that the words themselves have power, and the word order, verbs and repetitions have to be carefully tended if the text is to reveal itself on ever deeper levels.

A scriptural text is not just any story; it is a text that is divinely inspired, more alive in many ways than other tales. Its power is enhanced, deepened and accentuated within a community of hearers who believe. The hearers become the context: they live and breathe and feed upon the text, listening to it and cherishing it, hoping to make it flesh and blood, vibrantly alive in their own time and place. The story, the text itself, is handled like a Waterford glass, with utmost attentiveness and awareness of its value and worth. It is received as gift, an irreplaceable gift from a beloved friend, an heirloom passed down from generation to generation. Remembering that we are entrusted with it and that it will be passed on to those who come after us, we treat it with care, so that it will not be damaged, scratched or shattered.

In China there is a tale about the birth of writing.

* Once upon a time the Emperor Fushi was working on the laws of the universe. It was a taxing project, and it involved making sure that the boundaries moved and there was some give and take in all things.

One day a minor spirit who had been entrusted with historical records came up with a marvelous new invention. He had been hard at work recording history, all the events and happenings in the universe—no easy task. He had helpers, but the work was daunting. They had been tying knots in ropes for the passage of time and there was a rope for every place. It was slow going: so many knots, and so many ropes to keep track of. Remembering the knots was the hardest part.

He told the story of his discovery to the Emperor. One day he had gotten so overwhelmed and tired from his work that he just gave up for a while and went for a walk. The earth was new in spring and there was a freshness, a clarity to the air, to all things. He slowed down and breathed and began to watch small details in the trees, the buds newly formed, the sounds of the air moving around him. He sighed deeply and looked down. At his feet there were tracks in the mud, trails of footprints, paws, claws, feathers. Suddenly it dawned on him: of course—you could look at these prints and know who had come through, and when, and where they were headed; you could tell if they were young or old or injured or strong from these tracings and markings. There had to be a way that humans could make marks and leave traces too! He must make a set of signs that could be read as pictures for humans.

He began with simple figures, drawing everything. He forgot the ropes and knots altogether and went on short trips, drawing everything in sight. "Keep it simple," he kept telling himself. The drawings stacked up. There were pictures and sketches everywhere. He enlisted a friend to help him. She was especially good at small details that changed the designs, making them easier to understand.

Over time, the figures were developed and refined. Today, the characters resemble the original drawings and those who learn Chinese have to learn each character one by one. Learning to read and write in China is daunting work, but it is about communion, for all the many languages spoken in China share the same written characters. The characters make it possible to record history, to create written versions of stories that can be passed on, to capture meanings.

What follows is a story I first heard in just a couple of sentences from a friend returning from a sabbatical in the Orient. He was in love with this short story, based on something that actually happened in Japan around the eighth century. It is the story of one man's experience of coming to wisdom. The man's name was Tetsugen. His story, which is part of the Zen tradition of Buddhism, has been distilled over the centuries into an awareness for many peoples and traditions of the true meaning of words, books and scriptures—"sutras" in the original.

For many centuries, the wood printing blocks used for making pages of a book on the Buddhist sutras were available only in Chinese. Tetsugen, an eighth-century Japanese monk, dreamed of producing a Japanese version. He realized his dream, and the blocks are displayed in a monastery in Kyoto still.

Here is the way I tell the story, after having heard it from Ben Wren, Zen Master, long ago, and after having seen the print blocks myself in Japan and listening to a Japanese monk tell the story. The monk was conducting a tour for foreigners who were, for the most part, unfamiliar with Buddhism and Zen. He saved the print blocks for last, since they were considered the most valuable of all the treasures in the monastery's possession. I had been telling the story of the print blocks for over fifteen years before I heard the monk's version. I was stunned by the fact that, while his version was succinct and to the point, my rendering of it was so true to the core that we shared even certain phrases in our tellings.

＊   Once upon a time there was a young man who decided very early on in his life that he wanted to be holy. In eighth-century Japan life was hard for many people. Looking around, he realized that becoming holy, becoming enlightened was going to be hard too. So, in his youthful enthusiasm, he decided to take the shortest and most sure route. He decided to become a monk and left everything, embracing the discipline and committing himself to a master.

Life was good, but hard. Becoming holy was even harder. In addition to obeying the master and living in community, following the schedule of fasts, sitting and walking and chanting the sutras, he had to learn Chinese, because all the sutras, the chants and the scriptures, even the primary texts of the stories and *koans* were only in Chinese. As he set himself to learning the language, he decided that he had another ambition, another dream as well as the dream of becoming holy. He would find a way to translate the sutras into Japanese and get an edition printed so that the lay people of Japan could read, study and pray in their own language, and so, hopefully, become holier in their own lives, without the burden of having to learn another language.

He set himself to the task at hand and soon become renowned in his own sect, his own monasteries. He was ordained when still young and was made a master in his own right. And he began teaching outside the monastery, in small villages and towns, in great centers of learning, among businessmen, among government officials, anywhere. And he charged enormous amounts of money for his lectures and talks and saved his money. After just ten years he had enough money to hire a translator, buy and prepare the paper, and have the print blocks made. He would have his books.

But just as he was about to give the money to the translator and set the process in motion, a terrible famine took place in Japan. The rice crop was lost; the old and the children were the first victims, but soon even the healthy and robust were feeling the toll. There was no seed rice for the next crop. Tetsugen looked about at the suffering of the people and thought: How can I make books when the people who will read them are starving to death? And so he took all the money he had saved and, buying rice on the black market, gave away everything to the hungry.

As Japan recovered, he still had his dream and his energy was channeled into more talks, travels and begging. He begged from everyone and anyone. He was as gracious with the family who gave him a few coins as he was with the wealthy who gave him large sums. He still charged outrageously for his talks (though he also spoke to anyone who would listen as well), only this time it took a bit longer, almost twenty years to collect the money, because the prices for all the materials had increased. Finally he was ready with the translator and the carver of blocks and the paper. This time it was a typhoon that hit Japan that derailed him. Rivers were swollen and flooding the fields and wiping out bridges and roads. The food was destroyed and disease flourished in the rice paddies and streets. Once again, there was need for medicine, food, clothing and shelter for so many. How could he waste the money on books? And so, he took his savings and bought medicine, food, and materials for building.

Japan recovered and Tetsugen went back to his dreams. He taught, wrote, spoke, gave lectures, took on students, aligned himself with monasteries and begged shamelessly. But he was begging from those who had given before and he was often asked what he had done with the money they had already given him. This time it took nearly thirty years to come up with the money. All those years he prayed that nothing would happen so that his dream could become a reality: no cataclysmic upheavals, no disasters. And there were none. The translator was paid, the blocks were made, the paper was printed and the books were distributed to the people of Japan, for free—6,000 copies of the sutras, the prayers and teachings of Buddhism. Tetsugen was well into his eighties.

In the monastery there are many treasures, but this is saved for last: four small blocks that were used to print Tetsugen's books of the holy sutras. The monk tells the story and lets the guests look. And then he says: You know, there were three editions of Tetsugen's scriptures. The first two are far superior and more to be valued.

Words are to be cherished. Written and printed editions can be valuable, but the version to be treasured, honored and tended to first and foremost is that of the people, the flesh and blood folk who speak and hear and read the words and who are the incarnation of all the stories.

Here is a story from a text, familiar perhaps to more people. It is the story of Samuel, a young boy being called to be a teacher, wise man, truth teller to the people of Israel.

❋ The boy Samuel ministered to Yahweh under Eli's care in a time in which the word of Yahweh was rarely heard: visions were not seen.

One night Eli was lying down in his room, half blind as he was. The lamp of God was still lighted and Samuel also lay in the house of Yahweh near the ark of God. Then Yahweh called, "Samuel! Samuel!" Samuel answered, "I am here!" and ran to Eli saying, "I am here, did you not call me?" But Eli said, "I did not call, go back to sleep." So he went and lay down.

Then Yahweh called again, "Samuel!" and Samuel stood up and went to Eli saying, "You called me; I am here." But Eli answered, "I did not call you, my son. Go back to sleep."

Samuel did not yet know Yahweh and the word of Yahweh had not yet been revealed to him. But Yahweh called Samuel for the third time and, as he went again to Eli saying, "I am here for you have called me," Eli realized that it was Yahweh calling the boy. So he said to Samuel, "Go, lie down, and if he calls you again, answer: "'Speak, Yahweh, your servant listens.'"

Then Yahweh came and stood there calling as he did before: "Samuel! Samuel!" And Samuel answered, "Speak, for your servant listens." Then Yahweh spoke to Samuel, "Look, I am about to do something in Israel which will scare everyone who hears about it. On that day I will carry out what I told Eli regarding his family. All will be fulfilled from beginning to end. For I told him that I was about to sentence his family forever. He himself knew that his sons were blaspheming God, but he did not stop them. This is why I have cursed the family of Eli. Their sin shall never be atoned for by sacrifice or by any offering."

Samuel lay down until morning and rose up early. Then he opened the doors of Yahweh's house. Samuel was afraid to tell the vision to Eli, but Eli called him and said: "Samuel, my son." Samuel answered, "I am here." Eli asked, "What did Yahweh tell you? Do not hide from me. Fear the punishment of God if you hide from me

even one thing he told you." So Samuel told him everything to the end and Eli said, "He is Yahweh. Let him do
what seems good to him."

Samuel grew; Yahweh was with him and made all his
words become true. All Israel, from Dan to Beersheba,
knew that Samuel was really Yahweh's prophet. Yahweh
would appear at Shiloh; there he revealed himself to
Samuel by giving him his word. (1 Samuel 3:1-21)

We often hear this reading at the beginning of the year, in
Ordinary Time, before the coming of the Lenten season. The
passage is also often used in sermons and prayer services for
vocations. In practically all cases the middle portion of the
text is omitted—the part that details what Yahweh actually
spoke to Samuel about, the hard reality of what he had to tell
Eli. This word of Yahweh made young Samuel afraid, for it
confirmed what had gone before, the word that had come to
Eli, and it changed the future. Now Samuel was the prophet
of God, replacing Eli. The word now came to Samuel, and
through Samuel to the people of Israel. Samuel's life was no
longer in service to Eli, but to Yahweh and the nation that belonged to God.

The passage is more direct and more singular than many,
yet it follows the pattern of being chosen, being called—always in relation to the people. Samuel is young and does not
yet know Yahweh; "the word of Yahweh had not yet been revealed to him." The New American Bible translation reads,
"Samuel was not yet familiar with Yahweh," which gives another insight into the relationship between Samuel and God.
Samuel lives in the temple and sleeps in close proximity to the
ark of God. We are told in the previous chapter that he wears
the garments of a priest and is "growing in stature and worth
before Yahweh and the people"—a phrase that is used repeatedly in both testaments to describe someone who belongs to
God. In the early chapters of Luke's gospel it is used to describe Jesus' own development and life.

There is a sense that Samuel's service in the temple is a
prelude and that the primary work has not begun yet. Eli, his
master and teacher, is old. He is a prophet in Israel, yet it is a

time "in which the word of Yahweh was rarely heard: visions were not seen." It is a time of silence, of darkness, of no direction. Even Eli's own family has sinned; his sons have blasphemed. Eli has not had the nerve, the courage, even the faithfulness to rebuke his own children. He has neglected to teach or correct them. He has failed in his duty as a father in Israel and given example that is destructive and disrespectful of belief in Yahweh and his covenant commands. It is a time, then, of corruption, of lack of faith, of selfishness and oppression.

Nevertheless, we know from earlier chapters that Samuel comes from a family of faithfulness, of hope and devotion. His mother, Hannah, was barren and had been abused by her husband's other wife and family members. She prayed to Yahweh for a son whom she could give to the service of God. Her prayer is described (which means it is very important): "As she prayed before Yahweh, Eli observed the movement of her lips. Hannah was praying silently; she moved her lips but uttered no sound and Eli thought Hannah was drunk." The poor woman cannot even pray without being judged harshly and rebuked. She is "pouring out her soul before Yahweh" (her words in 1 Samuel 1:15) for she is in distress. She is beyond sound, going inside and down in her grief and need. And her prayer is answered. Samuel is vowed to the Lord before he is born, given as gift to speak the truth to a family and a society that mock and needlessly make others' pain more unbearable.

Hannah's song is recorded. A text is preserved of the words with which she aligns herself with all the abandoned and lost ones of the earth. When she sings she gives voice to those who are trapped and imprisoned by others, those who are maligned and judged inferior—even by religious people—because their pain is not respected or even noticed or acknowledged—except by God.

Samuel belongs to Yahweh from the beginning, but he is born of Hannah's longing and faithfulness and belief in God while others are about their own ways and lives, resorting to God only when they see fit. After Samuel is born, Hannah stands again in the presence of God (letting Eli overhear her prayer now) and sings strongly and rejoices and laughs, for she knows the power and the strength of her God: "Yahweh alone is holy, no one is like you; there is no Rock like our God...for Yahweh is an all-knowing God who weighs the deeds of all...and lifts up the lowly from the dust." In her experience of God, Hannah joins the prophets and liberators of Israel in a time of dishonor and forgetfulness of the covenant.

Samuel is called in his sleep. Three times he hears the voice, jumps up and obeys, even though he does not realize it is Yahweh who is calling his name. When he is told by Eli not to come to him, but to speak directly to the voice and answer, Samuel becomes the servant that listens to the voice of Yahweh and no longer to that of Eli. It is to Eli's credit that he understands what is happening and teaches Samuel what to do, how to pray and address God, and lets him go. It is even more to his credit when Eli hears what Yahweh's message is through this chosen child and responds: "Let him do what seems good to him."

Samuel, for his part, obeys: first his parents (the law) and his mother's vow; then Eli in service at the temple, jumping up repeatedly even in his sleep to answer as needed; and finally, Yahweh. Obedience must be learned before the word of the Lord can be understood or recognized, before there can be a relationship between God and an individual, before one can belong to God. It is God who gives Samuel his word and makes his words become true. His words have effect. And so Samuel, as young as he is, becomes a force to be reckoned with and listened to. The times have changed, and the word of Yahweh is now heard regularly. It comes through Samuel, but it was ushered in by Hannah, his mother.

All changes in history come from listening, from being a servant and from learning to recognize and be familiar with God. The call is more than just a call to a vocation. It is a call to belief and to practice in a world that often, even among believers, has no depth and no outward appearances of belief. The call is revealed in the plight of the poor, the hungry, the destitute, those whose humanity is not recognized because of biology or physical characteristics, and those who suffer doubly because of the treatment they get from "god-fearing" people.

The text is sparse, which is characteristic of all scripture passages, so every word is important. Samuel's answer to the voice of God is: "Speak, Yahweh, your servant listens." The response is direct and it reveals the quality of the core relationship as servant to Yahweh, a master unlike any other. It is in the present, continuing tense. It is an attitude, a way of defining oneself in relation to what is happening now: listening to the word of the Lord and acting upon it completely, utterly. Utterly—even the word expresses totality of expression, taken from the utterance and put into practice by the person who hears and obeys.

When Samuel listens he hears something that will make everyone afraid: what Yahweh is going to do, the gist of his words coming true in reality. Yahweh lays a sentence of judgment on Eli's family and that is the announcement, the first that the prophet Samuel must convey to others. Yahweh is with him, abiding, dwelling, as Samuel did in the tent, close to the ark of God. Now it is God who has moved in with Samuel, revealing himself to the people through Samuel. Samuel is servant and bridge. His life is directed by another, the other his mother cried out to silently and sang to so joyously. His only duty and responsibility now is to be the voice of God, speaking the words that he hears and obeys—the vocation of any believer at its ground root.

Here is another story, one with a bit of a twist. We are told by Jesus to remember this story and to tell it again and again throughout history. It is about a nameless woman. We know nothing about her except for one moment, one experience with Jesus. This version is found in Matthew 26:6-13 (also in Mark 14:3-9) and is wedged between two harsh texts: the story of the chief priests and the Jewish authorities gathering and plotting to trap Jesus and kill him and the equally discouraging story of Judas deciding in response to the incident with the woman to go off to the chief priests and leaders and sell Jesus for thirty pieces of silver. Jesus is surrounded by betrayal and lies, calculated destruction and evil—not just among his enemies, the authorities and leaders of the people, but even among his own trusted friends. The story must be read in that light.

* While Jesus was in Bethany in the house of Simon the leper, a woman came up to him carrying a precious jar of expensive perfume. She poured it on Jesus' head as he was at table. Seeing this the disciples became indignant, protesting, "What a useless waste! The perfume could have been sold for a large sum and given to the poor."

But Jesus was aware of this, so he said to them: "Why are you troubling this woman? What she has just done for me is indeed a good work. You always have the poor with you but you will not have me forever. She was preparing for my funeral when she anointed my body with this perfume. Truly, I say to you: wherever the Gospel is proclaimed, all over the world, what she has done will be told in praise of her." (Matthew 26:6-13)

There are so many interesting details about this story, the last story before the last supper, the preparation for Passover. First, Jesus never speaks to the woman. We know nothing about her except that she related to Jesus, knew Jesus and did something for Jesus that no one else had thought to do in just this way. In the story she approaches him, comes up to him and pours a jar of expensive perfume on his head! That certainly gets everyone's attention immediately. Even his own disciples are indignant, judgmental and harsh; they look only at what it costs and see a "useless waste."

What the woman has done has an ancient tradition: In Israel only priests, prophets and kings were anointed by having oil poured on their heads. The woman not only made a public act of faith, she proclaimed Jesus as priest, prophet and king in Israel for those who could see and hear: those who had heard his words and stories and had come to believe and see in him the presence of the word of God among them.

That is one interpretation. Jesus himself gives another: "She was preparing for my funeral when she anointed my body with this perfume." Jesus proclaims that what she has done is immediately connected to the reality underlying being priest, prophet and king: his death. After all, this was what Jesus was preaching just before coming to the house of Simon the leper. Just lines before he states: "You know that in two days' time it will be the Passover and the Son of Man will be handed over to be crucified." The others didn't hear, they weren't listening, but the woman heard and the words found a deep and responsive chord in her. She presents herself to him as servant and her actions speak on behalf of all those who have no voice. They hear clearly, they know who he is and they believe and follow him, even if the authorities and his own disciples are slow, resistant or refusing to see what is happening all around them: death and preparations for a murder. She offsets this with preparations for burial and anointing for glory.

Then Jesus makes a solemn proclamation—and he doesn't make many of these: "Truly, wherever the Gospel is proclaimed, all over the world, what she has done will be told in praise of her." She says nothing, yet sets in motion a story that has been interpreted in myriad ways, told in other places for other reasons and misquoted and used by all sorts of groups. The line most often interpreted is that of Jesus: "You always have the poor with you but you will not have me forever." Yet this sentence follows the words "Why are you troubling this woman? What she has just done for me is indeed a good work..." They are bound together in one thought.

There are two ways to go: One is that she herself is poor, wasting her saved, hard-earned jar of expensive perfume on a religious display of faith; the other is that it is Jesus who is poor, facing torture, rejection, betrayal and death and what she does for him is a good work: burying the dead with dignity and attentiveness. Jesus aligns himself with the poor. Whatever we do for the poor, we do in devotion to and worship of Jesus, for that is one of the primary ways Jesus has of remaining with us—"in the distressing guise of the poor," to use Mother Teresa's phrase.

But Jesus is interested first and foremost in questioning his own disciples and trying to teach them (and us, of course): "Why are you troubling this woman?" They are indignant at another's profession of devotion and faith. They are judgmental, protesting her behavior, her presence and nearness to Jesus, let alone what they feel is her "fault"—wasting the jar of perfume by not doing what they would supposedly do with it. They are belittling *her*, and Jesus is offended by their response to what she has done for him. He wants them to look at themselves and their own lack of devotion, of awareness of the tide of evil and decisions made against him. It is they who are ignorant, and there is a touch of indignation in Jesus' response to their behavior toward her, and toward himself and his situation.

Jesus' word is that this story is crucial. It must not be forgotten. It must be told, proclaimed throughout the world. It is part and parcel of the gospel itself: the good news to the poor, the word of God enfleshed in Jesus. This woman knows and expresses something that the disciples are missing and Jesus acknowledges that she is aware, she is right in her actions, and she understands his words more than they do. She is anonymous, but she is immediately familiar to anyone who understands Jesus. She is about doing a good work: attending to those who are preparing for death and funerals, especially those who die needlessly, alone or without comfort; those rejected by society, by religious people, by those who often consider themselves the disciples of God. She is about using all her resources in proclaiming the good news of who Jesus is, of personally attending to him, to his body, which is the body of all those who suffer, are tortured and killed with murderous intent and self-righteousness, all those who are not seen for who they are and are not treated humanely. This story is told in her honor and in honor of all those snubbed and rubbed out, all those with whom God sides, all those whom God hears and attends to when no one else has time or use for them.

In Matthew's gospel this encounter with the woman is the last episode before Jesus' celebration of the Passover. He goes from the house of Simon the leper and this anointing to a borrowed house for a last meal with his friends where he dips his bread in oil and gives it to the one who has betrayed him. The perfumed oil has become the oil and bread given to a betrayer. The story of the ointment that "could have been sold for a large sum and given to the poor" but was poured on Jesus becomes part of another, larger story. Jesus himself is sold for thirty pieces of silver. He becomes the poorest of the poor, one whom sinners and those who do evil in religion's name seek to murder, one who is betrayed by friends and left alone to die.

One story, only a few lines, and so many interpretations. But any of the interpretations must be translated into life, into decisions and priorities that have life, that are extended into the community. That is the reason for this story and for all stories. Stories by their very nature reveal the values, the dreams, the reality of those who tell them. They remind us of what is central to us and what we believe as well as of our failures and lacks, our losses and mistakes. They make community: we are known by the stories we tell, the company we keep and the words we repeat over and over again in worship, in singing, in prayer. We tell the stories again and again to enflesh the words in our time and geography, our bodies and good works. The stories are about transformations, about conversions, about changes that radically alter lives and history.

In his book for children, *Crow and Weasel*, Barry Lopez describes the journey of two friends seeking wisdom for their people as they learn from animals and seasons and places. "Remember only this one thing," said Badger. "The stories people tell have a way of taking care of them. If stories come to you, care for them. And learn to give them away when they are needed. Sometimes a person needs a story more than food to stay alive. That is why we put these stories in each other's memory. This is how people care for themselves." This is wisdom.

The stories in our traditions are life-lines, life-blood for people. They are a necessity of life and we must tell them. Many cultures and peoples believe that when poets, storytellers and singers (all artists) are lacking in a society, then that people is becoming extinct and beginning to act inhumanly. It is a dangerous time for a people when there are few truth tellers and proclaimers of the ancient wisdom, few left who practice the old ways of living.

There is a story told of the great rabbi Menachem Mendel of Kotzk. When his disciples asked him how he became a follower of the Hasidic movement, he was swift in answering. "There was a man in my town, an old man, and he told stories. Those stories persuaded me."

The answer surprised many of his disciples, and one said, "Oh, that man—he must have been an amazing storyteller, a great preacher and teacher or rabbi."

"No," said Rabbi Menachem, "he was a simple storyteller. But he told what he knew and I heard what I needed."

This idea is echoed by many. Joy Harjo of the Muscogee/Cherokee tribes says: I realize that what I'm doing is larger than I am. It has to do with the people and what the people need, what the tribe needs, more so than any particular or singular human choice. Joy Harjo is called a storyteller, but she considers herself a poet and a musician and she says: You know, stories are a part of that. In an interview with Joseph Marshall III in *Indian Artist Magazine* she adds that "I realized that I needed what poetry would teach me, which was to learn how to listen and to have grace. It's taught me a lot. I think it chose me. Sometimes I think poetry came up and said, 'Wait a minute, you poor thing, you are in need of grace; you need to learn how to listen; you need to learn how to speak.'"

She speaks of her tradition, the oral tradition:

> I think part of it has to do with the aliveness of oral tradition, the attention to speaking and knowing from the heart the power of the word. You know that words can change, can make things happen, can hurt people, can build up a community, and how you mean them and how you act out of them makes a difference. There's an awareness of that in the tribal communities, especially those who have kept alive their oral traditions and their cultures. You can tell students who have it and who don't, when there is an awareness of that sense. (p. 51)

Joy Harjo is a musician. With her band Poetic Justice she entertains, but she also informs and teaches. She goes on to explain her work:

> We are communicators. Poetry, particularly, communicates between worlds. I think one reason I came to poetry is, for me, it functions as a sacred language, so to

speak. In the tribes, the people who are involved in the most crucial and necessary ceremonies are the ones, often, who have the oldest words. They are the tribal poets...

I'm very aware of using English, of not having total command of my tribal language. In that sense, I'm aware of having to deal with structures that are different from tribal sensibility. Yet, when you write poetry or perform music, you follow the poetry, or the sound, back towards the place it comes from, which isn't bound by linguistic walls. (p. 53)

These insights and experiences are universal, learned and passed on to those who are seeking to be word masters, or to be mastered by a tradition of the word. She concludes by describing what she has learned in her journey as a poet:

How to not be afraid of what has to be said; to not be afraid of the truth, to not be afraid to speak it. You realize in the end it's not about you, personally, but it's about that thing that poetry is, the thing that painting is, what those things that touch our hearts and souls are...and so I feel like I'm in the service of poetry, in the service of people. (p. 53)

In the Jewish tradition, as well as in the Christian and other traditions, the primary prerequisite for a story, if it is to be true and to be worth telling, is that it be lived. The story is given to be transformed into an experience, into reality, into something that has power to transform people. Rabbi Carlebach says that the story is real in the moment of the telling and it strives for the "holy shiver" effect that reaches the soul. The story told and heard is another way of knowing, a mystical way of knowing. Elie Wiesel has said, "What does mysticism really mean? It means the way to attain knowledge. It's close to philosophy; except in philosophy you go horizontally while in mysticism you go vertically."

The soul has its own reality and stories take us there, into the deepest places, some of which have become blurred or misted over. Stories put us in touch with knowledge that we already know, but don't know we know, or have forgotten how to use. Words are passed on by word of mouth, from one person to another. The people are often carefully chosen, like Elijah and Elisha, Jesus and his disciples, the mullah and his followers, the shaman and her initiates, the storyteller and those who love the stories and are caught in the web. Once chosen, you realize that though you begin by listening to the word of another, eventually the stories are spun out of your very soul and being. You can't tell a story that you don't believe or that hasn't claimed you already, one that you don't practice. Ancient teachers in many traditions say that God hides in the stories; stories are where God takes refuge from the world that has become, hoping that someone will uncover and dream another more truly human world, closer to God's dreams.

The act of telling a story is a ritual. It seeks to transmit knowledge and pass on secrets of the heart and soul cherished by a community of people. It opens those who hear, who copy the stories and try to tell them, interpreting the secrets of the God that this community believes in and follows. And finally the story calls us to obey, to respond by making the story come true, through living it, through making the words take flesh in us. In the very down-to-earth words of Daniel Berrigan, "Faith is where your ass is" (not your head or your heart). It's where your words take you and where they make you stand. Each story you choose to tell defines and reveals. This is why we must choose our words with care, and our stories with even greater care. For those of us who claim to believe in the Word made flesh, our words are our truth. We will be judged on our words in practice, on how we have identified ourselves with the Word of God among us.

The story is told. After it is spoken aloud it is written down, annotated, put into other forms. Then inevitably it is interpreted, defined, codified, illustrated, put to music and shifted, sifted through other hearers and tellers. But whether it develops into a written word, a printed word, bytes on a computer, another language that crosses boundaries, cultures, religions—still, the story is in us. We are hieroglyphs, pictographs, and as the story moves through us it becomes altered, it becomes us and we become the stories we tell, the words we honor.

A closing story about the power of words, of ancient oral commands and power (all words and stories are really about power). It is called, simply, "The Druid."

❋ She was tall and tousled and the color of dusk settled about her face and the sort of light that comes from shooting stars dwelled in her eyes. But it was her hair that caught you: the raven blue-black of night and the richness of it, flying in the evening air like the birds going home, luring you to follow her there.

She was one of the old ones, a druid, and was more at her ease among the trees than among the children of earth, for the trees were known to be kind and mild, faithful, reaching for the highest points, and there was always a soft singing hidden in their leaves.

Here in the forest places she did not want for companionship, even of her own kind, and here she was immortal, deathless and undying. She did not know fear or terror or even loneliness, for she did not know love, a weakness that belongs only to those who will someday die.

One day it came to pass that another wandered lost into the land of oak and fir and evergreen and she looked upon the shadow that followed wherever this one went. She looked and gazed again, for she had never known shadows—she cast none as she crossed the ground whether in grand sunlight or in shade. She was not bound to earth, only to time.

She knew the laws intimately. To speak with one of these, an outsider, a stranger to her own kind, was to court death, to invite all the remnants of that outer world inside her. And so she walked silently behind, but kept her distance.

The stranger was hungry. She touched the trees and ate. She was thirsty, and she looked for a stream. There she bowed low with her face to the water's edge and an image emerged. The stranger gazed into her own eyes,

eyes that were familiar reflecting back from the stream, and she laughed aloud.

Fascinated, the druid too drew near. She had never seen her own face—but having no shadow, she had no reflection either. She stood forlorn and orphaned on the water's edge.

She had forgotten one of the laws—never to show herself to an outsider. The other spoke and asked directions. What was this place, and how could she find her way out?

The druid knew that here, now, if she did not speak, the stranger would enter her world. Unbound by time, the stranger would become like her, deathless and undying. But too, she would lose her shadow and her reflection. Then she knew terror, sadness, desire—or was it care or love? Wavering, she spoke and the stranger disappeared before her eyes.

Bewildered, she looked around and down into the stream. She saw her eyes like falling stars sparkling and saw too the shadow lying behind her on the ground. And then she knew...she had stepped over the boundary into time: the stranger dwelled within and the druid would die.

Always in the story is "the thing not named," the thing that is evoked piece by piece, slowly, given soul and tempting you into it, forcing you to hear, to wonder, to interpret, to decide. Willa Cather says: "Whatever is felt upon the page without being specifically named there—that, one might say, is created. It is the inexplicable presence of the thing not named, of the overtone divined by the ear but not heard by it, the verbal mood, the emotional aura of the fact of the thing or the deed, that gives high quality to the novel or the drama, as well as to the poetry itself." In more theological or religious terms it is the Midrash, the underlying truth, the inspired layers that are hinted at, that invite but do not force themselves upon us. They must be searched out, struggled with and taken to heart. It is, at root, the mystery that makes the story memorable, worth telling over and over again, and staking your life on.

Resources

The Art of Writing: Teachings of the Chinese Masters, trans. Tony Barnstone and Chou Ping (Boston: Shambhala, 1996).

Sven Birkerts, *The Gutenberg Elegies: The Fate of Reading in an Electronic Age* (Boston: Faber and Faber, 1994).

Kurt Brown, ed., *The True Subject: Writers on Life and Craft* (St. Paul, MN: Graywolf Press, 1993).

Gerald Donaldson, *Books* (New York: Van nostrand Reinhold Co., 1981).

Wen Fu, *The Art of Writing*, trans. Sam Hamill (Portland, OR: Breitenbush Books, 1987).

Joy Harjo, interview with Joseph Marshall III, *Indian Artist Magazine* (Summer 1996).

Georges Jean, *Writing: The Story of Alphabets and Scripts, Discoveries* (New York: Harry Abrams, 1992).

Barry Lopez, *Crow and Weasel* (San Francisco: North Point Press, 1990).

Manuela Dunn Mascetti, ed., *A Box of Zen (Haiku, Koans, Sayings)* (New York: Hyperion, 1996).

Graeme Rutherford, *Watchers in the Morning: A Spirituality for Contemporary Christians* (Victoria, Australia: Collins Dove/Harper, 1994). See especially the chapter "Conversion through the Word," pp. 61-81.

Burton L. Visotzky, *Reading the Book: Making the Bible a Timeless Text* (New York: Schocken Books, 1991).

David J. Wolpe, *In Speech and In Silence: The Jewish Quest for God* (New York: Henry Holt, 1992).

4

Words in Israel's Tradition

———— ✳ ————

One of the main elements of the tradition is silence . . . but we don't talk about it. (Eli Wiesel in a BBC TV interview)

"Is not my word like . . . a hammer that breaketh the rock in pieces?" (Jeremiah 23:29) As the hammer splits the rock into many splinters, so will a scripture verse yield many meanings. (Sanhedrin 34A)

"Black fire on white fire" (in the Midrash, the description of the Torah)

Here is a story from the oral tradition of Judaism. It is often told on the third night of the feast of lights, in early December.

✳ Once upon a time the land of Israel was sore beset by the Romans. The children of God were occupied, harried and persecuted relentlessly. Yet, as hard as life was, it seemed it could always be worse. The Emperor Hadrian issued a decree that it was unlawful, punishable by death to study the Torah or to teach it to others in any form. In fact, the Torah itself was condemned. To own a copy, to conceal a copy, let alone to honor it, dance with it or study it would bring torture and a terrible death.

But Rabbi Akiba defied the unjust law and continued to study. Finally he and some of his disciples fled into the desert where they could continue their studies without fear of losing their lives or of their families having to suffer because of their deeds. But the Romans heard of them and went after them. It seemed as though there was nowhere to hide, no safe place.

They cried out to God and complained to Rabbi Akiba: Why is this happening to us? What have we done? How can we keep on living this way, running at the slightest sign of a stranger, a sound, always looking over our shoulders, never at rest, never having any security? Of what use is it to keep on studying? What good is the Torah and its wisdom if we cannot practice it, if we do not know whether we will live through the night and be able to look at the next paragraph? Why are we so hounded by Rome? Why can't we be like the other nations and give up our studies and live in peace?

Rabbi Akiba listened with a heavy heart and then decided to tell them a story. Once upon a time, he began—open your ears, open your hearts and minds. Once upon a time there was a school of fish. They weren't very big fish and they were caught in a lake. Everywhere they fled, bigger fish pursued them. And, of course, from above there were fishermen with hooks and bait and nets always waiting for them to slip, to forget. It was a hard life, always looking for a place to hide, a cove, a reef, a patch of weeds. Finally they found a ledge, close to the surface but in a place surrounded by high rocks and dangerous outcroppings. They could breathe easily for awhile.

But while they were there, a crafty fox came along and saw them, thinking what a good meal a few of them would make. He sat on a rock and said out loud: "Oh, poor fish! What a hard life you have. Fishermen are everywhere and big fish and terrifying creatures of the deep are always after you." The fish listened and gathered close by. "You should come up here where it is safe, away from your enemies. Dry land would be safe" (they were just beyond his reach still).

But the fish listened and knew the trap. His words were true: partly. They answered back: "True, it would be safe on dry land. Living in this lake is hard, dangerous, but on dry land it is impossible to live. We would die immediately." And off they swam, a bit more content in their cramped place of freedom and hiding.

Rabbi Akiba looked at his frightened and tired disciples and said: We Jews are like those fish. We live in a lake. The Torah is our lake. It is hard, and dangerous. There are a lot of troubles here. But the fox is more dangerous. The fox is Rome. We are little fish. Life will be difficult and hard for us as long as we stay with the Torah and cling to its words. But without it, could we live at all? Without the Torah our life would be impossible. Remember that! And they clutched the scrolls to their hearts and continued to run and hide and study, giving praise to God, Blessed be his Holy Name.

Central to Jewish stories and the Jewish reverence for words—both the text and the accompanying commentary (Midrash)—is the notion of "tradition." According to Webster's Dictionary, the term means "the handing down orally of customs, beliefs, etc. from generation to generation." The secondary meaning is just as enlightening: "a story, a belief, etc. handed down in this way." The word comes from the Latin *tradere*, to hand over, to give, to transmit, to send directly. The notions of conforming to, enduring with and continuing, no matter what, are all included in this one verb. The emphasis is on "handing down or handing over"—from person to person in an intimate, immediate, conscious relationship of passing on so that the next generation is sure to have what is so cherished.

But the same word *tradere* is also the root of the word "traitor," to lead across and slander, to betray one's belief, one's friends, one's land. Those who honor a particular tradition are careful not to betray the core, the essence of what is handed on to others. What is given is rooted in a people, and what is given is essential to meaning, to survival and to the essence of who this people are and will become.

So many of Israel's blessings, commands and prayers begin with the words; "Hear O Israel," an ancient call to heed collectively what is happening and to become ever more a part of it. The text of the Torah records memory, history and design; the tradition is about handing on the power to interpret, to reflect on the text of the past as it is experienced in the present and so to make a future. The text is part of the conscience of the people. It is a deposit of riches to be dug into, mined and committed to memory, to be learned by heart in every age. The text and the oral tradition together create the vision and the future reality of the world.

The stronger the tradition, the more influence it has. A Jewish storyteller once told me that she makes *no* attempt to read a tale impartially; she translates everything into the language, beliefs and tradition of Judaism. She reminded me that every Jew in all times heard the Voice of the Holy One (blessed be His Name) giving (handing over) the Torah at Mount Sinai, yet each heard different sounds. The words resonated inside each according to his or her ability to hear and understand. Each can tell the story, or—better said—each can refract one insight, one way of hearing, one way of telling the story. Each can render a piece that the community needs for more complete meaning.

So each generation of Jews lives and breathes the stories and passes them on until there is a thread that connects each new generation to the ancient ones. The situations can change radically but the stories take flesh in all of them, thus bringing a Jewish history and meaning to all of time. The stories themselves are "on the go," much as Abram was called by Yahweh to "get himself out and to go forth" to a land that God would show him and his descendants. The covenant and God's words were to be found in all events, places, and relationships, carried by the nomadic peoples who became the children of God: Israel was to go and find God's meaning in all things.

Stories are mother-lodes of faith. To believe in the stories and to treasure them, handing them on to your children and to your children's children, is to pass on the faith, the identity of being Jewish. It is an unbroken string, tying together the ancient ancestors with contemporary believers. As Martin Buber says: "Judaism has not only a past; despite all it has already created, it has, above all, not a past but a future. Judaism has, in truth, not yet done its work, and the great forces active in this most tragic and incomprehensible of people have not yet written their very own word into the history of the world."

A page of the Torah is crowded with commentary, with the expressions of others' insights and discovered meanings throughout history. All are presented on the page so that newcomers to the text can benefit from the community's growing understanding, gleaned from the text and struggled with over years. The commentary, or embellishments to the stories, are called Midrash or *d'rash*, which comes from the Hebrew verb that means "to search out, to discover." This is the white fire which is the limitless song, story and belief that is in between, under, around and over, even laced through the black fire, the print on the page that appears limited and specific. The two together change everything! Simply described, the Midrash is the task or the adventure of reading between the lines of the text for the invisible stories that are hinted at in the words, phrases, repetitions, grammar, or style. The belief is that there is room in the text for lots more stories than the one on the page. So each page of the Torah is itself a dialogue, a conversation that keeps going on and on, between the original writer, all those who have read the text and taken it to heart, and the one reading it now.

The reading is not just imaginative or creative or whimsical, however. It follows patterns, principles and laws that have also been passed on traditionally to all Jews, especially to those dedicated to teaching the Torah. One of the primary principles is that "there is no before and after in the Torah," so chronology is not a constraint. It is taken into consideration, but all time doubles back upon itself and most of the enduring realities are consistent and forever. Thus, a line in Genesis can be intimately connected to one of the prophets or historical books: the reader, the student must be familiar with the whole and keep digging, noting details, discovering mysteries that are never ending. The Torah itself has no limits; the only limits are found in the ones who study and in their resistance to the depth of the mystery revealed.

There are always several levels of scripture to keep in mind. The first is *peshat* or *p'shat*, the black fire: the writing, the text itself, what is called the obvious meaning. This includes the standard commentaries on the page, along with the Torah text. And for anyone serious about the Torah, the words must be approached with reverence, with belief that the text is inspired. It is divine revelation. It is holy, and every "jot and title" must be taken seriously. There is always a reason—and sometimes there are many reasons—for the way the text appears on the page, even if the reason is not immediately apparent. In fact, if it is not immediately apparent, then that is a hint that something important is probably hidden within.

Reading each piece of scripture is like reading a piece of music and interpreting its nuances and resonances. There's the obvious "what" that it says, the plain sense of the passage and the meanings of the words themselves. Then there is the "how" of what is said; this is where the real work of interpretation begins. Some basics of interpretation: understand the context within another story, book, historical period, and so on. Remember that the text uses words carefully, sparingly, simply; it says as much as it can using finely crafted and carefully chosen words. Any interpretation must make sense, and the more it connects with other stories and passages, even passages written centuries later, the more sense it will make, the truer it will be. There is a beauty in truth telling that can be revealed in the interpretation as well as in the writing. It is important to dig and question, to study and find out what others have found. As the Sages say:

> "...all the words of this Torah. For it is no empty matter to you..." (Deuteronomy 32:47). Said Rav Mana, "For it is no empty matter to you, and if it is empty, to you (alone) is it so. And why is this? Because you haven't struggled with the Torah."

The struggle is a constant. Like breathing, sleeping, eating and praying, it is part and parcel of life for a Jewish believer.

Israel, the nation, is born of Jacob who struggles with a man (an angel, God) all night and seeks a blessing. After the struggle he is renamed Israel, who "is strong with God." Listen to the story, in connection to struggling with the scriptures.

✳ That same night Jacob got up and taking his two wives, his two maidservants and his eleven sons, crossed the ford of the Jabbok. He took them and sent them across the stream and likewise everything he had. And Jacob was left alone.

Then a man wrestled with him until daybreak. When the man saw that he could not get the better of Jacob, he struck him in the socket of his hip and dislocated it as he wrestled with him.

The man said, "Let me go, for day is breaking." But Jacob said, "I will not let you go until you have given me your blessing." The man then said, "What is your name?" "Jacob" was the reply. He answered, "You will no longer be called Jacob, but Israel, for you have been *strong-with-God* as you have been with men and have prevailed."

Then Jacob asked him, "What is your name?" He answered, "Why do you ask my name?" And he blessed him there. So Jacob called the place Peniel, saying, "I have seen *God face to face* and survived. The sun rose as he passed through Peniel, limping because of his hip. (Genesis 32:22-31)

The context is Jacob's return from Laban's tents and his going back to face Esau, with whom he has had no dealings with since he stole his birthright decades before. Both coming and going, Jacob has had dreams of angels and God. He has been full of fear and has prayed fervently for safety. He is about to meet face-to-face with the brother he has betrayed. He knows what Esau is: a hunter. For safety, Jacob sends his family and his possessions away. He will face Esau alone.

This is the way the text begins. Jacob is alone, alone with his memories, his sin, his weaknesses and all that he has learned since leaving home. Immediately he starts to wrestle with a man (or an angel) until daybreak. There is a sense of surprise, of no warning, no time to prepare or decide what to do. He must concentrate only on this man and wrestle with him. The word "wrestled" in Hebrew is *va-ye'avek*. The commentator Rashi explains it more as "twining, knotting or wrapping around one another, being tied together." Each is intent on pinning the other to the ground, of gaining ascendancy, of over-powering the other. This face-to-face confrontation is an experience of encounter that is passionate and exhausting.

The "what" is that they wrestle, they struggle for control. The "who" is a bit more tricky. Psychologically, is it Jacob's own mind and psyche grappling with what he has to face on the morrow because he hasn't dealt with what he's done all these years? The midrashic answer is that the other man is an angel, Jacob's guardian angel, not only his protector but the protector of his inner identity, his authority. And Jacob struggles with him for a blessing: forgiveness, a return to his own authenticity, strength to face his brother and his past deeds.

But there are other midrashic interpretations. One of them is that the angel is more than Jacob's guardian spirit; it is the guardian protector of Israel. Jacob is renamed after the struggle. When Jacob asks the name of the opponent who has blessed him, the reply is unexpected: "Why do you ask my name?" This suggests that Jacob already knows—his name is Israel. (Note: angels are often named for their task, or what they are sent to do in the world.) The angel is there to help him face what it has meant to be Jacob in the past and to release him from that, to introduce him to his new place in history, what he is to become: one of the ancestors of Israel, like his fathers before him, Abraham and Isaac. A new name entails more than a new identity. It is a wrenching free from the old life and a reorienting toward the future.

The text says that both prevailed, though Jacob knows that he just "survived." He limps from an injury that will remain with him for the rest of his life. Israel carries the old Jacob with him along with the angel's blessing. Soon this new person Jacob/Israel will be embraced by his older brother Esau and held face-to-face again. This time it will be Jacob who will pass on his blessing to Esau. But Jacob is crippled in a sense, bound to his past and what it has set in motion. Still, it is a blessing. He is bound now to his father, Isaac, who was once bound hand and foot for sacrifice. Jacob is bound to the covenant and the story will continue.

As believers in the scriptures, we are called to wrestle with the text, to wrestle with it face-to-face, all night, striving to prevail against its meaning. It gives its blessing and leaves us limping, facing the dawn with insight, awareness, a truer sense of our weakness and our strength, of the effects of our actions and deeds on all relationships. The struggle can change our names, alter our identities and give us something to pass onto others: either old blessings once stolen or new ones freely and humbly shared. It can give us the strength to avert violence in our lives, even violence that has resulted from our past evil and sin against others. It can give us a new way of walking, limping—an inbred deep-in-the-bone awareness of self, of God and of meaning.

We have to be stubborn and stay with the text and not give up or let go before we have been given something to hang on to—even if only more words! Listen to the teaching of one of the old storytellers and teachers, Rabbi Nachman:

> Rabbi Nachman taught: one must be extremely stubborn in the service of God. Every individual, no matter how great or small he may be, must undergo a seemingly endless number of ups, downs, and disappointments before succeeding in God's service. Sometimes the very forces of heaven seem to cause him to become discouraged and make him want to give up. Often he finds that only through clinging stubbornly to what he has set out to do can he gather strength to continue; but this takes an extremely great amount of stubbornness. Remember this advice well; its uses are many. (Gedaliah Fleer, *Rabbi Nachman's Fire*)

Struggle with the text is based on faith, faithfulness and holy resistance, hanging on for the blessing to be given. It is a dialogue with other believers and with the Holy that is hidden in the night of the text and in the light of the spaces between words, lives and events. It is a way of praying, of pushing God to be faithful and of pushing ourselves beyond our present level and practice of belief. We are part of the divine plan and covenant. God initiates the struggle, engaging us in long periods of intensive, single-minded and single-hearted reflection and study. It is an arduous process of taking responsibility for our behavior that either serves to hasten the plan's actuality or sidesteps it and seeks to avert it. Jacob is alone. He has separated himself from all that he possesses and holds dear. When he leaves the place of struggle, limping, he has also been corrected by God. Interestingly enough, another translation of the name Israel is "corrected by God," revealing God's intervention into history, into the lives of individuals and peoples. Jacob's story is about Israel, about the future and about how God works in the lives of all people, but works definitely in the lives of his own people who believe in him. And this presence that struggles with the Jewish people abides through all generations.

If we read earlier and later passages in the text, we learn that the god of Peniel was responsible for putting people on the right road. His prophet was Balaam (Numbers 22–25), who gave warnings to those who passed through his territory. Balaam also contended with an angel (he was saved by his donkey) and became a prophet who honored Yahweh, giving a blessing that announced a "star of Jacob" who would be King David, chosen by God to begin the rule of God in Israel.

There is a story I tell to demonstrate how a parable works. I have heard it told as an English story, as a European story and as a Jewish tale. Basically they follow the same form and pattern, although there are small shifts in details and interpretations. The Jewish version goes something like this:

❋   Once upon a time there was a holy and scholarly rabbi. He was brilliant. In fact, he knew the answer to every question, to any question anyone could ask him. He traveled from town to town, teaching, telling stories and answering questions. Once he arrived in a town and, after much preaching and answering questions, a young girl cried out: "I have a question for you, Rabbi, and I'm sure you can't answer it."

The rabbi smiled and said: "Ask."

She spoke: "I have a bird hidden behind my back, held carefully in my hands. Is the bird dead or alive?" Already she had thought up a way to come up with the answer that would be the opposite of whatever the rabbi said: "If he answers 'It is dead,' then I will let it go free and if he answers 'It is alive,' then I will crush it in my hands and take its life from it."

The rabbi knew the young girl was intent on tricking him, especially in public. How could he answer and yet still give her some dignity too? And then in a moment he was given the answer. Tears came to his eyes, partly in gratitude, but in knowledge as well. He had difficulty speaking, getting the words out. He answered her: "My dear child, you hold the bird in your hands. The answer all depends on you. You can let it live, or you can take its life. The answer is in your hands."

You see, the rabbi knew immediately the larger implications of the girl's question. In her hands was the fate of the Jewish people; every person, even every child, holds a portion of that fate. But the bird is also the destiny and the future of all humankind. What each of us grasps in our hands is more than anything we consciously know. What struggles for life in our grasp is not unimportant, but crucial for others' survival. What each person does or does not do contributes to either life or death; to *tikkum olam* (repairing the world) or to its destruction.

Maimonides, a great Jewish scholar and lawyer, said that we should see the world as a scale, balanced and equal. Any action, any word, any choice can tip the balance one way or the other. Every person makes a difference and what happens to one affects all the others. Nothing just happens. Or, as Viktor Frankel put it after the Holocaust:

We who lived in concentration camps can remember the men who walked through the huts comforting others, giving away their last piece of bread. They may have been few in number, but they offer sufficient proof that everything can be taken from a man but one thing: the last of the human freedoms—to choose one's attitude in any given set of circumstances—to choose one's own way.

That "way" for any member of the Jewish community is rooted in tradition, in continuity, in stubborn faithfulness and searching, struggling for a way to give glory to the Holy One in spite of whatever is happening. It is belief in a promise handed on and written into all the unwritten texts of the Torah, the lives of believers, belief in the invisible yet discernible presence of the One who is faithful, who walks with Israel.

In any text, what appears to be missing, lacking or absent, is in reality there, waiting to be uncovered. Meaning is scattered throughout the text, in between the words and stories. It is an underground spring seeking someone to chance upon it.

A way of looking at the text is found in Martin Buber's description of the way to look at the law. "The true meaning of love of one's neighbor is not that it is a command from God which we are to fulfill; but that through it and in it we meet God. Existence will remain meaningless for you if you yourself do not penetrate into it with active love and if you do not in this way discover its meaning for yourself. Everything is waiting to be hallowed by you. If you wish to believe, love!" We must love the text, the words of the scriptures, in order to arrive at any depth of understanding.

Loving means hanging on, not just in facing the text, or in hearing the stories, but in all circumstances of life and encounters with others. Meaning is there in everything! The Talmud tells a story about even Abraham needing to learn to endure, to be patient, to wait on God and others around him. It is said that an old man was passing through the desert and came upon Abraham's tent. He was welcomed, served and fed. He was offered all the extensions of hospitality. After eating, Abraham invited his guest to pray with him to the one God. The man refused. He informed Abraham that he had another god: he was a fire-worshiper. And with that Abraham drove him from his door. Later that night Abraham finished his prayers and went to bed. And God, the Holy One, appeared to him in a dream saying: "Abraham, Abraham, I have put up and borne with that ignorant man for seventy years! Couldn't you have put up with him, suffered him patiently for one night?"

What we learn in Torah study needs translating in every other area of life. That is part of the richness of the Midrash, the stories and songs, and the oral traditions of the Jewish people: what is learned must be translated into life, extended into other areas. All the stories, all the texts are meant to be more than words, or commands, or insights. They are meant to be ethical, transformative, moral ways of dealing with reality. They are to be made into *mitzvot*, spiritual practices that carry out the commandments. In fact, telling a story or listening to a story is considered a mitzvah in a Jewish community. It is a way of praying, of being inspired and encouraged to be holy. Every story, all study of the text is to be followed by the words: "therefore," or as storytellers often say: "The story begins when the teller stops talking." What follows the story, the studying, matters as much as the telling and the devotion to the words. All those who hear are supposed to remember that stories save and that they were meant to hear this particular story and take it to heart.

It is said that when people tell stories, even God comes to listen. This isn't unusual, because in the Hasidic tradition God created man and woman because he was lonely and wanted to tell his stories to us. God too is entranced by our stories. In fact, listen to these words: "Those were the very words of those who fear Yahweh. Yahweh listened and heard what they said. He ordered at once that the names of those who respect him and reverence his Name be written in a record [book]" (Malachi 3:16). In fact, the rabbis believe that one of the ways God keeps holy the Sabbath when he rests is to study the Torah. He prays and looks for stories to listen to. He eavesdrops on those who tell!

There is a story told of the Seer of Lublin.

✳   He was passing through town and saw a great light shining from the synagogue. He smiled and knew that inside there were probably a number of scholars hunched over a page of the Torah, studying long into the night. God was being praised and the sparks of light were being strengthened in the world above and below. He detoured and went inside, only to find that there were two men sitting talking at a table, no scholars and no Torah. He asked them: "What were you talking about?"

They looked at each other, reluctant to say. But he pressed them.

They answered: "We were telling stories about the deeds of the *tzaddikim* (the saints)."

The Seer left, continuing on his way, knowing that he had learned something important. He now knew that storytelling produced the same kind of light and holiness that studying the Torah does. As he walked now he told himself and the Holy One all the stories he knew.

Stories, all the riches of the oral tradition, operate like Torah study. Every time a story is told there is a meaning. No matter how many times you hear a story, there is something else in there. There is a *teshuvah*—a return, something new that is given back, something stirred by the teller, something touched in the listener. We learn by listening, over and over again, like praying. The oral tradition is carefully guarded and transmitted. It is a honor and a responsibility to tell the story the way it was told, the way it was passed on. And in listening and learning to tell, we stay open to the power of the Spirit, the Voice that comes through the "white fire" as well as the words. The power of the story is in the faith of those who speak and those who hear. This faith provides an openness, a possibility of conversion, a space where miracles can happen.

Listen to this tale.

✳ Once upon a time Rabbi Moshe Isaac of Kelm (19th century) was preaching in the synagogue. It was a holy time, just days before the high holy days of Rosh Hashana and Yom Kippur. It was the time of reflection and self-examination and communal taking of responsibility for all that had been done or left undone in the past year. The blessings and the judgment of the year to come lay seeded in those days of repentance and confession. The city of Bialystock had a rather large Jewish community. There were synagogues for different trades: leather workers and tanners, tailors, shoemakers, carpenters and bricklayers. The rabbi was teaching in the tailors' synagogue. And he was telling a story. They had heard it before but they loved the way the rabbi told it. He was full of passion, emotion and intensity as he detailed heaven, the judgment throne of God, the orders of angels and the town of Bialystock itself. He thundered forth, listing and defining what the town was noted for: its strengths and talents, its gifted people, its weakness and lacks, the quality of its prayers, fasting and almsgiving. It was an examination, a sort of public record. Then he launched into the discussions of the scholars and sages in heaven as they debated the fate of the town of Bialystock this year. He got to the part about the judgment and cried out that this was the moment of judgment, the moment of truth. There was no escaping it now. The angels cried out: "Tailors of Bialystock arise, stand before the judgment seat and hear your sentence this year." And immediately every tailor in the synagogue stood trembling. They were ready for the judgment. The words of the story were the reality. Just as chronological time isn't a constraint, so too geography and place have loose boundary lines in the storytelling moment. (A version of this story can be found in *Storytelling and Spirituality in Judaism*.)

The story continues the people's beliefs and hopes, their dreams, memory and history. In the story—in the Torah, the words and the oral traditions—lies the depth of life and the possibility of the future coming true, coming through them. It is a long chain of study and prayer, of survival with grace and freedom.

Here is another story that says it in another way. A much longer version can be found in Zalman Schacter and Howard Schwartz's *The Dream Assembly*. (Note: a *tallit* is the prayer shawl worn for worship, both in private and in public, by all Jews. Often a *tallit* is handed down within a family.)

＊ Once upon a time a student asked a rabbi after the morning prayers: Tell me, Rebbe, who wore the first *tallit*?

The rabbi's eyes shone. No one had ever asked that question before, but he knew the answer and it was close to his heart, for he was Hasidic and had been told by his master. Of course, it was our ancestor Abraham who wore the first *tallit*. The angels who came to visit him with the Lord gave it to Abraham as a gift for his hospitality. It was woven of light, the light of the *shekhinah* (the Holy One in exile), made of glory and hemmed with the blue of the heavens for it drew together all that is below on earth and all that is above. It was, of course, Abraham's most prized possession. He passed it on to his son, Isaac, and then to Jacob, and then Jacob in his old age handed it over to Joseph. Joseph's coat, which made his brothers so jealous, was in fact, the first *tallit*, the one that had been given to Abraham, for it shone with the colors of the rainbow. His brothers bloodied it and gave it back to Jacob.

But Jacob gave it to Joseph again. And when Joseph died in Egypt he was buried in it, for he knew that there would be four hundred years of exile before his people were home again. When Moses led the people to the promised land, they carried the bones of Joseph, still wrapped in the *tallit*. And by a miracle it was still intact. Moses took it and kept it for himself, until he passed from earth, giving it to Joshua, to Aaron, to Eli, to Samuel and to King David and Solomon. It was a gift along with the covenant. It always had that other light to it.

But then the temple was destroyed. Some think the *tallit* was returned to the world above, but others say it was passed on, that it moved around. It was the mantle of justice passed to Elisha by Elijah and then passed to Shimon bar Yohai who wrote the Zohar while wrapped in it. It has been given to those who teach, who immerse themselves in the mysteries of the Torah and who share the knowledge that brings deeper understanding of the law and compassion to all who suffer. They say it once was hidden in the synagogue where the Golem was fashioned in Prague and of course, the Baal Shem Tov wore it until he gave it to his daughter Odel, who gave it to her daughter Feige, who gave it to Reb Nachman of Bratslav.

The *tallit* travels, they say, with the people, seeking out the ones who lead the souls and kindle the sparks in every generation. The rabbi had no sooner finished his story when the disciples were on the edge of their seats and jumping up and down, for Reb Nachman was of the generation that had preceded them! Where was the *tallit* now?

The rabbi continued: "Some say he was the last mortal to wear it until the Messiah comes, but others say no, it will continue to journey with the people."

Here the story endings diverge. According to one ending, the rabbi's eyes shone. His students looked at him, waiting for the story to continue, but he said nothing. Then he turned and gestured for them to follow. They left the study hall and went to the rabbi's house, into his room, where he knelt before a chest and opened it. The light spun out into the room and their eyes were dazzled. According to another ending, the rabbi said nothing and gave the *tallit* to his disciple who took it with him. One of the many rabbis who perished in the Holocaust had it with him, but, of course, he gave it to a storyteller, one who carried the tradition, the Torah, in his or her soul. Today, somewhere in the world, that first *tallit*—woven of light and blue thread—is picked up every day and night. Someone puts it on and prays for the Messiah to come, prays for strength and faithfulness for the Jewish people and prays for that light to dwell in all those who hear the Voice still and thrill to its words and hidden meanings. So they say.

Resources

Avigdor Bonchek, *Studying the Torah: A Guide to In-Depth Interpretation* (Northvale, NJ: Jason Aronson, Inc., 1996).
Yitzhak Buxbaum, *Storytelling and Spirituality in Judaism* (Northvale, NJ: Jason Aronson, Inc., 1994).

Sterna Citron, *Why the Baal Shem Tov Laughed: Fifty-Two Stories about Our Great Chasidic Rabbis* (Northvale, NJ: Jason Aronson, Inc., 1993).

Lawrence J. Epstein, *A Treasury of Jewish Inspirational Stories* (Northvale, NJ: Jason Aronson, Inc., 1993).

Shalom Freedman, *In The Service of God: Conversations with Teachers of Torah in Jerusalem* (Northvale, NJ: Jason Aronson, Inc., 1995).

Louis Ginzberg, *Legends of the Bible* (Philadelphia, PA: Jewish Publication Society of America, 1975).

Meyer Levin, *Classic Chassidic Tales* (Northvale, NJ: Jason Aronson, Inc., 1996).

Barbara Rush, *The Book of Jewish Women's Tales* (Northvale, NJ: Jason Aronson, Inc., 1994).

Zalman Schacter and Howard Schwartz, *The Dream Assembly* (Nevada City, CA: Gateway Books, 1989). Pages 69-72 contain a version of the *tallit* story.

Howard Schwartz, *Miriam's Tambourine: Jewish Folktales from Around the World* (New York: Seth Press, Macmillan, 1984). See also other collections by Schwartz.

Avivah Gottlieb Zornberg, *The Beginning of Desire: Reflections on Genesis* (New York: Image, Doubleday, 1995).

5

The Word Made Flesh

Story as Person

———— ✳ ————

Look carefully around and recognize the luminosity of souls. Sit beside those who draw you to that.
(Rumi)

What good is it to me if Mary gave birth to the Son of God fourteen hundred years ago, and I do not also give birth to the Son of God in my time and in my culture? We are all meant to be mothers of God. God is always needing to be born.
(Meister Eckhart)

How to speak of a story that comes true, of a word that becomes flesh, of truth who becomes incarnated, of a person who is the story that lives forever, having being raised from the dead, no more to die? So much of the Christian tradition seeks to put into words belief in a Word that defies limits and boundaries, a Word that surpasses language, a Word made of flesh and blood, a Word that one knows, loves and stakes one's very life on. The Book of Revelation, the last in the Christian scriptures, sings forth:

I saw a new heaven and a new earth...
I saw the holy city, and the new Jerusalem...

> You see this city? Here...
> he will make his home among them;
> they shall be his people,
> and he will be their God;
> his name is God-with-them.
> He will wipe away all tears from their eyes;
> there will be no more death,
> and no more mourning or sadness...
>   (Revelation 21:1-5, Jerusalem Bible)

Since the birth of this human being, Jesus of Nazareth, born of the carpenter Joseph and his betrothed wife Mary in a cave in Bethlehem, writers have sought to explain who this man is for them and for the whole of humanity. St. John Chrysostom in the fourth century speaks of his birth:

> And how shall I describe this birth to you? For this wonder fills me with astonishment. The ancient of days has become an infant. The One who sits upon the sublime and heavenly throne now lies in a manger. And the One who cannot be touched, who is without a body, now lies subject to human hands. The One who has broken the bonds of sinners is now bound by an infant's bands.

Writers, scholars, preachers, poets, singers and spiritual guides speak of a human being, Jesus the Christ, "the firstborn of all creation" (Col 1:15) who is the singular focus of history, the heart of God's own love. The apostle Paul speaks of the Christ in terms that are awesome, eloquent and divine: "He is the image of the unseen God, and for all creation he is the firstborn, for in him all things were created, in heaven and on earth, visible and invisible... All was made through him and for him. He is before all and all things hold together in him" (Col 1:15-17).

Two thousand years later, a Franciscan friar, Stephen Doyle seeks to explain this in a tape recording, quoted in an excerpt from Jack Wintz's book *Lights: Revelations of God's Goodness* in *America* magazine.

Throughout this talk, Father Stephen smuggles in such little comments as "There is nothing in this world that makes sense apart from Jesus Christ" and "Whatever exists in this world was made for the sake of Jesus Christ." Later, he waxes poetic: "If we looked around and listened to this world about us, and if the singing birds could be formed into a chorus and the rustling breeze and tinkling rain could have a voice and the roar of the ocean could be put into words, they would all have one thing to say: 'We were made for the sake of Jesus Christ.' "

Father Stephen also offers a good answer to the riddle: How can it be that Christ, who came after Adam and Eve, nonetheless came before them in God's thinking? How can the Incarnate Word be the first and the last at the same time? Borrowing a popular analogy found in St. Francis de Sales' *Treatise on the Love of God*, Father Stephen explains it this way:

> If you wanted to make wine, what would you do? First of all, you would have to plant a vineyard. Then you would have to fertilize the vines. You would have to trim them. Eventually, you would harvest the grapes, press them and let them ferment. Finally, you would get some wine.
>
> What was the first thing on your mind? The wine. What was the last thing you got? The wine.

In the same way, Jesus' arriving late on the scene, notes Father Stephen, does not contradict his holding first place in God's mind at the creation of the universe. Christ is the first and the last, the Alpha and the Omega. (Wintz, pp. 22-23)

This man Jesus, born in history during the Roman occupation of Palestine in the first century, has even influenced the way we designate time in the Western world: B.C. before

Christ and A.D. after Christ. In the twelfth century Bernard of Clairvaux, a monk in France, wrote of him:

> For when I name Jesus I set before me a man who is meek and humble of heart, kind, prudent, chaste, merciful...and this same man is the all-powerful God whose way of life heals me, whose support is my strength. All these re-echo for me at the hearing of Jesus' name. Because he is a man I strive to imitate him; because of his divine power I lean upon him. The examples of his human life I gather like medicinal herbs; with the aid of his power I blend them and the result is a company like no pharmacist can produce.

And in this century, the artist/writer of the South, Flannery O'Connor, is quoted as saying: "The artist, if he is doing his job properly, can hardly fail to testify to the consequences of God becoming incarnate, even if only by way of presenting the destruction, the evil, where he is rejected."

This one human being has been "the cause of the rise and fall of many," not only in the Israel of his day, but also in governments and nations throughout history ever since. The opening of Matthew's story of Jesus of Nazareth begins with a genealogy that goes all the way back to Abraham, proclaiming Jesus as the Messiah, the long-awaited one in the memory and hope of the chosen people of Israel and the son of David. The closing words of the story are a commission to Jesus' disciples to reach out to every part of the world with the good news of freedom, forgiveness, justice and the presence of God on earth forever. The passage portrays a paradoxical mixture of human disbelief and faith:

> As for the Eleven disciples, they went to Galilee, to the mountain where Jesus had told them to go. When they saw Jesus, they bowed before him, although some doubted.
>
> Then Jesus approached them and said: "I have been given all authority in heaven and on earth. Go, therefore, and make disciples from all nations. Bap-

tize them in the Name of the Father and of the Son
and of the Holy Spirit, and teach them to fulfill all
that I have commanded you. I am with you always
until the end of this world. (Matthew 28:16-20)

This person and the stories he told have given heart and
hope to generations of people struggling for justice and dignity. They have given his followers the courage to offer mercy
and forgiveness in the face of persecution, torture and death.
Archbishop Oscar Romero, the bishop of El Salvador who was
shot while celebrating the liturgy in 1978, spoke in a homily
just days before his death: "But let us remember that Christ
became a person of his people, of his time; he lived as a Jew;
he labored as a worker in Nazareth and, ever since, he is
made flesh in all people. If many have moved away from the
church, it is precisely because the church has been a little
alienated from humanity. But a church that would feel as its
own all that is human, and would wish to incarnate within itself the sorrow, hope, and anguish of all who suffer and re-
joice, that church would be Christ loved and awaited, Christ
present. And that depends on us."

The belief of the Christian church is that this man Jesus is
the Son of God, the Word spoken by God as hope and balm for
humankind. Jesus is still present, vital and alive in the scriptures, in the stories he told and the accounts of his life, in the
people who believe in his words, and especially in the poor of
the world. The care we give to "the least of our brothers and
sisters" reveals how we honor and worship Jesus (Mt 25:31-46).

The voice of God is clear and distinct for those who have
ears to hear and hearts that believe and lives that strive to put
into practice his own way of "announcing good news to the
poor" (Lk 4) until the kingdom of God, the kingdom of peace
and abiding justice, comes in its fullness to all. Dom Helder
Camara, the archbishop of Recife, Brazil, now in his late eighties, reminds believers: "We must have no illusions. We must
not be naive. If we listen to the voice of God, we make our
choice, get out of ourselves, and fight nonviolently for a better
world. We must not expect to find it easy; we shall not walk

on roses, people will not throng to hear us and applaud, we shall not always be aware of divine protection. If we are to be pilgrims of justice and peace, we must expect the desert." The voice of God spoke to us through none other than God's own beloved Son, a suffering servant and healer who, though crucified and killed, was raised from the dead to sit at the right hand of God the Father. How did this man's life become the basis for Western civilization's understanding of what it means to be human, made in the "image and likeness of God"? A story that is close to the oral tradition gives us some idea of how this could have happened. The story is found at the end of Luke's version of Jesus' life, chapter 24.

* That same day, two of them were going to Emmaus, a village seven miles from Jerusalem, and they talked about what had happened. While they were talking and wondering, Jesus came up and walked with them, but their eyes were held and they did not recognize him.

He asked, "What is this you are talking about?" The two stood still, looking sad. Then one named Cleophas answered, "Why, it seems you are the only traveler in Jerusalem who doesn't know what has happened there these past few days." And he asked, "What is it?"

They replied, "It is about Jesus of Nazareth. He was a prophet, you know, mighty in word and deed before God and the people. But the chief priests and our rulers sentenced him to death. They handed him over to be crucified. We had hoped that he would redeem Israel.

It is now the third day since all this took place. It is true that some women of our group have disturbed us. When they went to the tomb at dawn, they did not find his body; they came to tell us that they had seen a vision of angels who told them that Jesus was alive. Some friends of our group went to the tomb and found everything just as the women had said, but they did not see him."

He said to them, "How dull you are, how slow of understanding! You fail to believe the message of the prophets. Is it not written that the Christ should suffer all this and then enter his glory?" Then starting with Moses and going through the prophets, he explained to them everything in Scripture concerning himself. (Luke 24:13-27)

This is the beginning of the story, but it is also a story within another story. It begins in the present, with two men, obviously friends who have been in Jerusalem during this terrible week of destruction. They are concerned with only one thing and this is what they are talking about as they head for Emmaus, for home. They are going back where they came from. They are running away from the experiences of loss, pain, destruction, murder, politics and—worst of all—lost hope in someone who they thought would be the one to set Israel free from oppression and injustice. It's a seven mile walk, but it will be a long walk back, because they are leaving behind their dreams and what they staked their hopes on.

As they are walking, Jesus falls in with them, but to them he's just another stranger on the road—and an ignorant stranger at that. He asks them questions and gets them to talk, to share their hearts and bare their souls. When they realize that he seems unaware of what has happened in Jerusalem, the city of God, the center of Jewish worship and life and hope for the Messiah, they halt in distress. This is the outside rim of the story.

Now we move to an inner layer. The two tell the story of the man they had followed: Jesus of Nazareth, from a town of no import, a town of riffraff, drifters, poor itinerants and mercenary soldiers, a rough town. The man was a prophet, one who spoke the word of God to the people, reminding them of priorities. He spoke of the covenant that set them apart and claimed them for God. He spoke of the law that held them bound together, showing forth to all other nations that God dwells in the midst of those who are just and who care for those on the fringes of society, that God's presence is palatable in the quality of human relationships. This man was a prophet mighty in deed and in word before God and all the people. In preaching and teaching, in exhortation and truth telling, in forgiving, healing and exposing lies and injustice and hypocrisy, he was always honoring God. But his message was not heard by the nation and the leaders and people; he was put to death. Worst of all, he was handed over, betrayed into the hands of his enemies in his own religion, his own society and he was condemned by the authorities and crucified. He died ingloriously, ridiculed, humiliated, shamed and despised by all.

The next line reveals how heavily the two on the road had invested in his words and message: we had hoped that he was the one to redeem, and save and set us free. This is the crux of the inside story: lost hope, dreams deferred, a wound that is raw and bleeding still. Together they are leaving behind the horror of a good man murdered and publicly accused by his own, in collusion with the nation's enemies.

But here comes another story—hearsay—from women who belong to their small group, the remnant left after the leader's death. It's been three days since his execution and burial and the Sabbath is over. Early that morning, when the women had gone to the tomb to finish the burial and mourning rites, they couldn't find his body! Not only that, they told an astonishing story about a vision of angels who said that he was alive! Of course, some of the group headed off to check out this preposterous tale. They found everything at the tomb exactly as the women had reported, but him they couldn't find a trace of. They had lost hope. They refused to believe, to listen to the women's story.

These two made a decision to leave, to put it all behind them: the man and his message, his life and his death, their belief in his dream of the kingdom and their hope that some of it might come true and they would be a part of it.

Jesus has heard the story, his story from their experience, and he wastes no time in giving his take on the events that have happened. He scolds them—not too gently—reminding them of reality, of their own history, of all that the prophets have said about the Messiah, the one who would come. He asks them a question: Was it not necessary that the Messiah should suffer these things and then enter into his glory? They should know better, if they know the ancient prophecies and the old stories. They are like those who believe half-heartedly and so remember the good parts of the story and try to ignore the pieces that are not so easy to remember and pass onto their children and friends.

And so Jesus tells them again of their story, the story of a people, of Israel and of God, beginning with Moses, going way back to the original liberator and law-giver of the people. He tells them a long story, emphasizing all the parts that have to do with him: the hard parts as well as the promise of glory and honor. Oh, to have heard the story that they heard! Oh, to have had the memory and to be able to tell the story back. This story lives in the oral tradition of Christianity—it has not been recorded, but it's out there and is a basis for what this story of Jesus became: the Word of God made flesh, the one who became the story. Jesus goes through all the prophets— Elijah and Elisha, Samuel, Nathan, Amos, Hosea, Jeremiah, Isaiah, Ezekiel, Micah, Baruch—and he pieces together a story that makes the miles fly by. They walk seven miles, but in no time they are at their destination. The story in the text continues:

❋   As they drew near the village they were heading for, Jesus made as if to go farther. But they prevailed upon him, "Stay with us, for night comes quickly. The day is now almost over." So he went in to stay with them. When they were at table, he took the bread, said a blessing, broke it and gave each a piece.

Then their eyes were opened, and they recognized him; but he vanished out of their sight. And they said to each other, "Were not our hearts filled with ardent yearning when he was talking to us on the road and explaining the Scriptures?" (Luke 24:28-32)

It appears that the storytelling is over and the storyteller is going on his way, but they press him to stay. They don't want the words to end, they don't want him to depart, for their hope is restored! It's evening, the dark is coming on, and they have been walking with the light all these hours and many miles. He is easily persuaded (almost as though he was waiting to be asked), and so joins them, stays with them a while longer. They sit down to eat. As they continue their talking and discussion, the man does something familiar, something they remember from their own experience and from stories told to them. He takes bread, blesses it, breaks it and hands it around: he acts out the ritual of the great Passover story, the story of freedom from slavery and Egypt, the story of blood smeared on doorposts and the angel of death passing through as those ready to escape break unleavened bread and drink wine.

But there is another story, a much more recent ritual celebration of this Passover story. The night before he died, this man Jesus dined with his friends and disciples. He broke bread and blessed it and gave it around, though he did not partake of it himself, and said "This is my body given for you"; and with the cup, "This is my blood, a new testament, a new covenant, binding a new relationship between friends." He had fed crowds often before. This night, the last meal he was to have with his friends, was steeped in old memories and songs, prayers and rituals, with a new twist. Now he was dead, and there was a strange tale of his body being gone and angels proclaiming to frightened women that he was alive.

The blood has been shed, poured out, and the body has been broken and torn and now this man is doing what Jesus did! When they look closely at the man, he is gone! Vanished from their sight. The bread has been eaten, his body is within them and the story is ringing in their ears and burning in their hearts. It is stirring in their souls, helping them to remember, to see and understand what they had been blind to before in their grief and fear and bitter disappointment. They look at each other and they are filled with feeling. They overflow with wonder at what has happened to them and what this could mean to others, the friends that they have left behind. They have to go back, to tell their new story to the others. And that's what they do.

* They immediately set out and returned to Jerusalem. There they found the Eleven and their companions gathered together. They were greeted by these words: "Yes, it is true, the Lord is risen! He has appeared to Simon!" Then the two told what had happened on the road and how Jesus made himself known when he broke bread with them. (Luke 24: 33-35)

We can imagine them retracing their steps to Jerusalem, nearly running, discussing again all that has happened and the ramifications of the story actually coming true! They burst in on the Eleven who—as we know from other stories—are locked away in an upper room, in fear and trembling themselves, hoping against hope as the story unfolds around them, touching them and receding as waves on a shore. The two are greeted with the announcement of still another story: he has appeared to Simon, the one who betrayed him and ran off and didn't see him die—he's appeared even to him! And that story isn't told in the text either. What a story that would have been—of forgiveness and healing, of stumbling attempts at expressing love and wonder and being beside oneself with fear and hope.

There is a saying among storytellers: All stories are true; some of them actually happened. Belief in the truth of the story is crucial to the listeners' participation and belief, to being drawn into the tale and becoming a part of it as it is told again. This story is true, but what if it actually happened and is happening now? What does a story like this do to all the other stories: the old ones and the ones yet to be told?

After they hear of Jesus' appearance to Simon, the two tell of their particular encounter and story—what happened on the road: the stories Jesus told them while they were on the way, the acting out of the story in the breaking of the bread, and the moment when their eyes were opened, when they knew who he was and what he was saying. Then poof—he was gone. Vanished. What a day, what a night! Words flying back and forth, people moving back and forth, coming together to listen, to hear and to tell good news that could barely be believed.

But the story isn't over yet! It gets even better!

＊   As they went on talking about this, Jesus himself stood in their midst. (And he said to them, "Peace to you.") In their panic and fright they thought they were seeing a ghost, but he said to them, "Why are you upset and why do such ideas cross your mind? Look at my hands and feet and see that it is I myself. Touch me and see for yourselves that a ghost has no flesh and bones as I have." (As he said this, he showed his hands and feet.)

In their joy they didn't dare believe and were still astonished. So he said to them, "Have you anything to eat?" and they gave him a piece of broiled fish. He took it and ate it before them.

Then Jesus said to them, "Remember the words I spoke to you when I was still with you: Everything written about me in the Law of Moses, the Prophets and the Psalms had to be fulfilled." Then he opened their minds to understand the Scriptures.

And he went on, "You see what was written: the Messiah had to suffer and on the third day rise from the dead. Then repentance and forgiveness in his name would be proclaimed to all the nations, beginning from Jerusalem. Now you shall be witnesses to this." (Luke 24:36-48)

They tell the story with wonder and passion and intensity, wanting to believe what is happening to them. In the middle of the telling, the story comes true again: Jesus appears to them. He is there and speaks the line that will become the essence of all the stories of resurrection and new life: "Peace be with you." These are the first words of the story of what he has been through: life, betrayal, crucifixion, death and resurrection—and he is alive! There is peace: abiding joy, harmony, rightness in the universe. There is blessing and meaning, a sense of serenity and hope despite all the horrors and disappointments of life. He is with them, and the reality of peace— *shalom*, wholeness and holiness—is alive and with them. It is here. It is true. They still have trouble believing and coping with this radical shift in their sense of reality: that death is not the final word: peace is! Jesus eats with them and befriends them again. He seems intent on making them touch the story, touch the words in his flesh and blood and bone. He holds out his hands and commands them to touch him. Oddly enough, the text doesn't say whether or not they did or if anyone did. It is another story perhaps.

Jesus begins again to interpret the story of his life. He tells it from his vantage point, the way he wants them to remem-

ber it so that they can tell it when he vanishes again. He tells
the story again so that they can tell it in shared breaking of
bread, in a community that gathers to eat together and to
break open words and hearts as theirs were opened by him.
He sends them forth to tell all the world this story, the only
story worth telling. Start here, in Jerusalem where it happened, and go—go everywhere and speak in your joy and belief, and in the telling he will be present.

I often use this story, as long as it is, with churches in
parish missions during the Easter season, the seven weeks
following the feast of the Resurrection. I do not read it; I tell
it as a story. I have learned the words by heart and it flows, it
mesmerizes them. Sometimes, often even, people are stunned
into a stillness that eventually breaks into loud, excited and
stuttering words and reactions. And when that happens, after
the silence, people say that their hearts were burning, their
hopes rising and they had the sense, often for the first time,
that Jesus somehow is present. He is sensed and there is understanding, insight mixed with fear and wonder and wild
hope: What if this is true? My God, what does that mean for
me, for my story? The experience is almost impossible to describe but in the telling the presence of Jesus becomes real.
The community knows and comes together to share the
hopes that are coming back to life. And that is followed by interpretation, their way of hearing the story and what it
means to them; they discover pieces they had missed before
and there is startled recognition when someone says something that they suddenly remember, something that is part of
their own experience. The words are often jumbled. Many
voices at once are trying to say something that they now
know is true about themselves, about others, about suffering,
death, loneliness, God, the need for others, bread, companions on the way.

At that point I often have them break into small groups
and tell the stories they think Jesus might have told to those
on the road. I ask them to pick a prophet, a psalm, a piece of
the story of Moses and the Exodus and tell that story and see
what it means in light of this story. What does it say about resurrection, the conquering of death by passing through death,

trust in Jesus' God, the Father, and reliance on the Spirit of Jesus that is given in the blessing of peace, in the words of the gospel, and in the retelling of the old story. The stories are fascinating: funny, insightful, engaging, full of hope. There always seems to be more to tell, more to hear, and more to take in hand and make come true in our own lives.

This story absorbs other stories and casts them in other lights. God is near, as close as our hearts. God is hidden in words, lurking in every gathering of those who speak about the possibilities of hope, of life stronger than death and of the sheer power of love to transform suffering into forgiveness, reconciliation and new forms of life. Not only is God near, God is passionately concerned about injustice, about the suffering of the innocent and the poor, the marginal members of society and those we ignore or treat inhumanly. The Word of God commands us unerringly to be caring of certain people, to be kind to them and hospitable, but—above all—to be just and human, loving them as we claim to honor God in our midst. This God is intimately concerned about history, about violence and inhumanity; this God will not simply stand by.

The story of Jesus gives the power to change all the endings so that finally there will be judgment, justice and peace. All the hopes of humankind will one day be fulfilled and there will be life in spite of all the death and despair we might experience. The story says that God's Word, the Word that was a sigh over the chaos, became flesh, became human. Then and ever since, the possibilities of what can come true, of how we can come true, are limitless. We are invited into divinity, into community, into the Trinity that is the home of the Word made flesh that still dwells among us.

Just recently, in the encyclical *Redeemer of the Human Race*, John Paul II has written:

> Jesus is the center of the universe and of history (#1)...Christ the Redeemer fully reveals human beings to themselves and if we wish to understand ourselves thoroughly...we must draw near to Christ... In Christ and through Christ, human persons have acquired full awareness of their dignity, of the heights to

which they are raised, of the surpassing worth of their
humanity, and of the meaning of existence. (#10, 11)

The person of Jesus is the core of the oral tradition that
undergirds the texts of the gospels, the early writings of the
church and the writings of the fathers and mothers of the first
six centuries of Christianity. The stories of conversion, of faith,
of belief despite persecution and martyrdom, of communities
that sought to live without distinctions of "Jew or Greek, slave
or free, man or woman, young or old, rich or poor" are born
of reflection on the texts. They are born of listening to the stories of those who believe and what they have learned from
their own and others' experiences of commitment, loss of faith
and forgiveness and reconciliation, and unbounded love expressed to all, even enemies, in the name of the Son of God,
Jesus the Christ.

Just that one word, the Name Jesus, is fraught with the
power to convert, to transform and to divinize people. A practice that is at the heart of spirituality and prayer in the Russian traditions of the Eastern Orthodox Church reflects the belief that the breathing in and out of the name of Jesus itself
makes one holy and unites one with the very heartbeat of
God. The ancient prayer, "Lord Jesus Christ, have mercy on
me a sinner," is repeated over and over one thousand times a
day, breathing in on the first portion and breathing out on the
second. This practice gradually affects one's mind and stills it.
It quiets the body, bringing peace and a profound awareness
of one's actions and words, and finally sinks deep into the
heart, taking up the music of the universe, the song of the angels and spirits and gathering all those who seek to honor
God in Jesus Christ. Somehow one is united not only with the
name, but with the person of Jesus Christ and the Body of
Christ: all those made in the image and likeness of God.

The sound of the Word, the sound of the scriptures, especially when spoken aloud and in a group, has an effect that is
revolutionary and transformative. Even when read aloud
alone, however, it has curative and positive effects. Here is a
story told from the early days of the church in the desert.

❋ Once upon a time there was a young man who came to an old hermit in the desert and asked him: "How can I become holy and happy quickly?"

The old man replied: "It's easy. Just go to one of those caves over there and take your scriptures with you. Read them night and day and you will find what you are seeking."

Off he went and obeyed and came back in three days. "How is it going?" he was asked.

"Terrible," he said, and he complained that it was boring and his mind was wandering and he didn't remember much of what he was reading and didn't understand it either.

The old man smiled at him and said: "Don't worry, you're doing just fine. Go back and keep reading every hour of the day but add one thing to your practice: get a basket and fill it with sand and set it outside the entrance to your cave. Every morning and each evening go to the spring and get a bucket of fresh water and pour it over the sand in the basket. Come back in about seven days and tell me how you're doing."

Off the man went and obeyed, and returned at the end of the week.

"How is it going now?" the old man asked.

"Still terrible. I drift off constantly, and I don't understand anything more than before."

"What about the sand?"

"Oh, that—I pour water in, just as you told me. Some of it leaks out of the basket and some of it pools at the top and some sinks down into the sand."

"Good," said the old hermit, "you're doing just fine. Go back and continue, and return every week to tell me how it's going."

Off the man went again. He did as he had been told and every week he came back with the same report. Nothing was happening at all.

One day, however, he came and announced that something had changed: all the sand was gone from the basket!

"Good," said the old hermit.

"But I'm just as unholy as before and now I'm pouring water into a clean basket."

"Yes," said the old man, "and the same thing is happening to you, you just don't know it yet. You see, you are the basket and the Word of God is the water that you've been pouring over the sand: the sand of your sin, your needs and lacks, your weaknesses and pride, your unhappiness and selfishness and impatience. The basket doesn't remember which drop of water washed away which grain of sand, but the sand can't stand long against the water. And you won't remember which word washed away which sin or weakness, but all that needs to change in you will be transformed. Your soul can't stand long unchanged against the water of the Word. Go home now and live your life, but keep pouring the Word of God over your life and some day you'll know what it's like to be the clean basket, empty and open, and ready to carry life and bread, or something that another needs."

These stories—the stories of scripture that are told aloud, told by heart, the spin-offs from the text—are the oral tradition that is somehow close to the person who is the Word made flesh, the person whose spirit and power lie in the words uttered in the air and shared by others. And all the stories say the same thing: come true, be like God, holy and bound to others in compassion and justice, not fearing even death for I am with you and will be until the end of time. Life will win out. Truth will win out. Stake your words and your life on mine, for:

> The Spirit of the Lord is upon me, He has anointed me to bring good news to the poor, to proclaim liberty to captives and new sight to the blind; to free the oppressed and announce the Lord's year of mercy. (Luke 4:18-19)

And that year of the Lord's mercy is every year for those who tell these stories. Here are two new stories that are steeped in the tradition of the Word as person, Word made flesh that not only comes true, but brings life to others. The first is about a young woman. It is called "The Fisherwoman."

* Once upon a time, when the earth was very young, there lived a woman who chose to dwell near water. There was a village nearby and the people survived through the seasons and years by tending their fields and setting out their nets to fish. The woman had been born in the village, but with time she had to move farther and farther away from it.

For, as all the young children were learning the crafts and trades of the village from their teachers and elders, she discovered that she had a very special gift. Instead of setting out nets to catch the fish running up stream, she would spend long hours looking into the water's face until she could see the fish. Then, at exactly the right moment, the fish to be caught would come up to her waiting hands. She would catch the fish in her bare hands. And, strangely enough, what she caught was always adequate for her and her family's needs with a bit left over to spare for a visitor's meal.

All the villagers soon heard of this. She tried to explain this new way of catching fish to her friends, and then to the elders of her tribe. But everyone laughed at her and mocked her. After all, they had been setting out their nets in the old way for years and had always gotten more than enough fish. In fact, they had caught so many fish that they had scattered the leftovers to the dogs and on their fields to help the crops grow. Besides, this new way was stupid and time consuming. What good could come from waiting and wasting endless hours watching the water, hours that could be put to better use elsewhere?

The girl didn't have any special gift, they decided; she was just lazy and slow-witted. And in great sadness, as more and more of the villagers mocked her, she moved farther and farther away from the houses and spent more of her time watching the water.

Then, one day, after much thought about the matter, she decided to break with her tradition and her people and move to another village downstream. Perhaps there the people would understand and take her in. And so she moved on, settling in the next village, helping with the crops, teaching the children and living like everyone else. But always she would return to sit at the water's edge, resting at its feet, letting her eyes move over the water.

In the mornings she could be found there before the sun glanced across the water. She would watch the mist dancing softly on the water's surface, followed closely by the outstretched arms of the sun. Or before a storm she would run quickly to stand in awe before the changing waters being chased by the hands of the wind which brushed rudely past trees and limbs, restless and violent in its movements. And, rain-wet, turned almost to water herself, she would wait for the sighing wind and dying storm to retreat, leaving the water laid out calm and beautiful again before her.

At sunset she would come to watch the sun play tag with the water spots and rainbows on the surfaces of the small waves. And when the darkness spread its cloak over the water leaving only a huge dark mass of unknownness, she would carry away the sparkle in her eyes and the mystery in her heart.

She knew when the fish ran, when they came to frolic with each other. They would eye her, jumping in the air in the soft mornings and late afternoons. She knew which belonged to her clan for food and which belonged to others, which needed to make it through the nets so that they could live to spawn again. And whenever her village set out the nets, she inwardly protested at so much unnecessary death. The catch was indiscriminate.

Finally, she could hold her tongue no longer and she spoke. She told them of the other way to fish, of standing still and gazing and taking with their hands only the fish they needed. But, as in her home village, they laughed at her and told her to leave them alone.

And so it was in many villages, until finally in her sadness and aloneness she returned to her own village. She had changed. But they had changed too and they had long ago forgotten about the strange woman who caught fish by looking through the water and waiting for the fish to come into her hands.

As she looked at her people, a greater fear and sorrow came on her. They were tired, slow moving, hungry and without laughter. No one welcomed a stranger into the village. She would just be another mouth to feed and they had so little themselves.

She painstakingly traveled the overgrown path to her old house by the water. No one had been there since she had left so long ago. Once again she heard the water calling to her and, obedient, she went to water-sit and gaze into the places where she had really always lived. And she sat at home, there, for a long time.

Very slowly, she came to see that the water too had changed. It was murky, slow, stagnant and lifeless. Her heart began to hurt. She had lost her gift and could no longer see through the water. Gradually, to her horror, she realized that she had lost more than her gift of water-watching. She had lost the fish. There were none in the water. And she began to weep.

Then in her sorrow she understood the lifelessness of her village and knew the fate that awaited all the small and great villages she had visited in her journeys. She began to weep again—this time for her people who had lost so much through their carelessness and ignorance. Even she had not really seen the value and significance of her own gift and the need to share it with others. She needed to learn to feel as much tenderness and appreciation for her own people as she had for the water, for the fish and for her gift for catching them. And so she cried, but this time not for herself, or for her lost gift or even for the water and the fish long dead, but for the villagers, her own people.

And as she bent over and cried, unable to stop, with her tears falling steadily into the languishing waters at her feet, something mysterious happened. As the tears entered the water they moved and darted, flashing for a moment of light before swimming off as fish. The tears streamed from her eyes, like old waters crashing down waterfalls, and the fish multiplied till the villagers, hungry and desperate, saw the gleaming fish leaping once again in their waters.

This time they remembered the strange words of the woman who had lived in the village long ago. They watched the fish and gazed at the water alive with gracefulness and newness. They sat still with waiting hands and the fish came, as they once had come to the girl.

The woman sits, it is said, by the water's edge, alone and weeping still, keeping her people alive, learning the truth of her gifts. And so it is said in the ancient wisdom sayings: What you catch and take for your own can be returned by compassion alone. So it is today that we sit at the water's edge with the rest of the village in this season when the fish run, watching the water and learning to see in true compassion and wisdom. So, children, learn to fish well and remember the woman who caught fish with her bare hands.

The next story is based on actual historical events reported on British radio in 1976. Tony Cowan, who wrote the story, calls it "The Time-Keeper."

＊ Decades ago in the coal mines of northern England there were scant safety measures to protect the men, boys and ponies that worked in the mines and the loss of health and life was common. Sometimes the only thing that stood between a miner and death was the sheer brawn or agility of his mates. Sometimes what was called for was self-sacrifice. Labor was cheap, but human life never was.

It happened that one day there was a massive cave-in which trapped twelve miners behind a wall of fallen rock and debris. The seam of coal they had been working on was the deepest and least accessible in the whole mine, and now the entire tunnel between them and the exit shaft was blocked.

When the coal dust began at last to settle, the men called out their names and most said they were not seriously injured. They quickly ascertained that no one had been caught underneath the falling rubble. It was also clear, though, that they were completely sealed off from the rest of the mine. They could not even hear the emergency siren that was sounding through the lift shaft above them. They could only wait and hope. One man suggested that they start digging away at the debris blocking the passageway, but another said that if they did that they would use up the oxygen too fast. All they could do was sit down and wait for rescue from above. Suddenly, every man down there had only one thought: will they reach us in time?

As the twelve sat waiting in the darkness, a voice called out, "Timekeeper! Can you tell us how we're doing for time? How long do you think we can last in here?" The timekeeper's voice sounded clear, decisive, and strong: "It was ten thirty just before the accident. There's twelve of us and about fourteen feet to this pocket we're in. If we keep still, we've got two hours of oxygen, by my reckoning. We'll be all right. We'll be fine." No one questioned him or doubted his words. They just hoped, listening to each other's breathing, trying to detect any sound of digging from the other end of the seam.

Time passed. They waited. At intervals, someone would call out, "Time!" and the timekeeper would announce, with a momentary flare of a match, "Fifteen minutes" or "Just ten more, lads." The periods between announcements seemed to get longer and longer, and yet the keeper always marked off small increments, never more than twenty minutes. At certain moments it seemed every man was asleep, but no one was.

When at last it seemed that only minutes of oxygen remained, the sweet sound of hammering and digging was heard through the rock and rubble. Rescue, after all! No one called out for the time because they had been keeping count of the minutes and clearly the two-hour deadline was just then being crossed. A few of the men tried to cheer, but their voices caught weakly in their throats. Several cried. Finally, a draft of air and a shaft of light from a lamp broke through to them.

Of the twelve men who had been trapped in that coal seam, all but one survived. The one they carried out was the timekeeper. When they made it to the surface, they were greeted with cheers and weeping from other miners, wives, and relatives who had rushed to the mine when word of the disaster had reached the town. The town priest was there and immediately called them to prayer for the man who had lost his life in the incident. Tears of relief were mixed with sorrow and consternation; why had the timekeeper alone died? The priest exclaimed, "The miracle is that any of you survived! You've been trapped down there for over six hours!" Drawing the pocket watch from the timekeeper's vest, one of the surviving miners saw that it had been broken in the accident. The hands on the watch face were stopped at ten thirty.

Compassion and life, life given for others: these are the stories of the tradition of Christianity. It is a tradition kept alive in the telling and in the lives of those who believe that the Word made flesh still dwells among us, that we too are the story, and that we can come true.

Resources

Marcus J. Borg, *Meeting Jesus Again for the First Time: The Historical Jesus and the Heart of Contemporary Faith* (San Francisco: Harper, 1994).

Claus Bussmann, *Who Do You Say? Jesus Christ in Latin American Theology* (Maryknoll, NY: Orbis Books, 1985).

Flannery O'Connor, quoted in *Images of Grace*, ed. Harold Fickett and Douglas R. Gilbert (Grand Rapids, MI: Eerdmans, 1986).

Robert J. Schreiter, ed., *Faces of Jesus in Africa* (Maryknoll, NY: Orbis Books, 1991).

John Shelby Spong, *Liberating The Gospels: Reading the Bible with Jewish Eyes* (San Francisco: Harper, 1996).

R. S. Sugirtharajah, ed., *Asian Faces of Jesus* (Maryknoll, NY: Orbis Books, 1995).

Jack Wintz, "Christ, the Head of Creation," *America*, September 14, 1996, pp. 22-23.

6

Tellings, Teachings, Parables, *Koans*

———— ✳ ————

God speaks as softly as possible, and as loudly as necessary. (Rafi Zabor)

You can see heaven through a needle's eye. (Japanese saying)

The tapestry of life's story is woven with the threads of life's ties ever joining and breaking. (Rabindranath Tagore)

How does one learn? How does one teach? Silence, word, experience, solitude, relationship, dialogue, a slap with a wooden sword, questions that appear crazy but have innumerable revelatory answers, stories whose endings drop you through a trap door into a subterranean cavern, statements that are both beautiful and dissonant—anything that can turn the world of the disciple upside-down. All of these are good places to start!

This chapter will deal with the story, the parable, the Zen *koan*, the Sufi dictum: all the oral traditions that pass on not only knowledge, but enlightenment and the experience of conversion. In this form of oral tradition, anything is fair! The pursuit of wisdom is a journey, whether one takes it by walking, dreaming or following a Way. As the Spanish poet Antonio Machado says: "Travelers, there is no path; paths are made by walking." In more ancient words, St. Augustine said the same thing: "*Solvitur ambulando*" (It is solved by walking).

A story only about twenty years old begins us on the path.

❋ Once upon a time, in the days long before the emperors and mandarins ruled China, the power and the wisdom of the land came from the wise ones who lived in the mountains. Their authority and truth-telling was universally recognized and even simple folk planned their lives around a visit to a wise one so that they could ask one question. These wise ones lived perched high on the mountains, looking out in silence at the towering peaks and the empty unknown chasms. And it was from long looking and dwelling amid the mountains that the wisdom came.

Now, during this time, there lived a man who had been born in the mountains. He was poor and unlettered and had known the wise ones as if they were his own relatives—they dwelt so near to him. But he was not wise. He was just a simple man who worked at the trade his father had taught him when he was young. He spent his days and nights carrying other people's baggage up the mountains so that they could make their pilgrimages without having to worry about the trail and everyday necessities. But this man had a dream. Someday, if he worked very hard at his trade, and took extra trips up the mountain, perhaps he could put enough aside to retire early and build himself a small and very simple hut to live in. Then he could sit and watch the mountains himself and perhaps gain some small portion of wisdom before he died. He lived on this dream. And he learned the mountains well, the paths and the trails, where to find water, where to rest and spend the night, the dangers and pitfalls, the unknown and never-visited places.

Every morning he would begin again, with his dream alive in his heart. He would bend over and lift the baggage onto his shoulders and start the long slow journey up the steep mountainside. He would closely watch the path, lest he fall off a cliff, or stumble over a rock, or twist an ankle. He remembered that he, too, dwelled in the mountains, but the only time he got a chance to see them was when, weary from the climb, he stopped to rest, laid down his burden and took a hurried glimpse at the beauty all around him. And the years went by this way for him, as he bent to pick up other people's baggage and carry it up, then down the mountain trails.

Then one day, around his seventy-third birthday, he began to realize that his dream would never materialize. He was growing old and feeble, and the trips up the mountain were harder, more painful and slower. And he had not managed to save any money, or build a hut or even to find a place to start. At night he was so tired from his struggle up the mountain carrying all that weight that he would fall asleep immediately. Then he would rise early the next morning and go right to work. He became disheartened. He had no dream to live on anymore. He thought of trying something else, but what did he know about anything else? Nothing. He was good only for carrying baggage up a mountain. There was nothing else before him, but to spend the rest of his days doing that. He realized he would never get the chance to sit and watch his treasured mountains and learn wisdom.

And sadly, without heart, he arose the following day to meet his next traveler. Bending over, he picked up the baggage and once again began the arduous trail up the mountain, watching for rocks and gullies and hidden dangers along the way. But, this time, he saw the trail with old eyes, eyes that had grown more comfortable with the path and suddenly he realized he knew a lot more about the mountains than he had thought.

He knew where water was, the fresh and quick running kind. He knew the best paths to take, the shortcuts and the longer ways that presented grand vistas of the horizon. He knew where to rest under tall trees that gave shade from the climbing sun. He knew too, long before others, the telltale signs of the changes of the seasons. And he knew the tender things too—where the flowers grew in the mountain meadows and when the birds sang their solitary and unknown songs. He knew the dangers that others could so easily fall into unawares. He knew where all the wise ones lived and where no one had ever dwelled before. He knew the path that wove through the mountains as gracefully as a web woven by a spider but invisible until the dew on it was touched by the morning light.

The journey somehow didn't seem so arduous this time. And when he arrived at his resting place and bent over to put down his burden, he straightened up and looked around. Once again he reveled in the magnificence of the peaks that soared above him and the majesty of the rock and massive stone that rose cathedral-like all about him. He looked at the mountains as he always had, in awe, but now saw them, not as smaller, but as truer than before. He knew then that his mountains were great and mysterious too, and that the path that rose up before him, that had kept him bent and bowed, had also shared its significance with him. The spires of the mountains were no less majestic than before, but the simple, silent and unnoticed signs of the mountains were clearer and more finely etched into his spirit.

His fellow traveler returned from speaking with the wise one, ready to return to the valley below. And the man bent over once again, bowing to take up the burden of the baggage on his stooped shoulders. But this time as he began his journey down the mountain, he smiled. It was the smile of a man who had lived long in the mountains and had grown wise.

A parable, a very gentle parable to ease us into the search for wisdom and truth. In the East the search is old and noble, and the searcher can take many paths. "There are many paths. They all lead into the forest—where they disappear. Learn about the forest!" (Zen saying). But keep in mind the warning to beginners: Nothing is as it appears to be. In Japan and China, India, and Tibet, Buddhism has left a long mark, influencing both the oral and written traditions of the various schools. The emphasis has always been on the experience of passing on enlightenment, of truth-telling and becoming, rather than on writing. The various forms of writing, even the calligraphy itself, is meant to catch you up and hold you, drawing you in to study a character's presentation as well as its meaning. Sayings, *koans*, parables, poetry, stories (sutras), are all bases of the oral tradition; so are *ikebana* (flower arranging), archery, *sumie* (ink painting), swordsmanship, the making of silk, pottery (especially *raku*), *kabuki* (theater). In fact, most art forms are part of the oral tradition, taught not so much through a Western sense of logic or rationality, but through discipline and through doing.

In contrast with the long parable above, the succinct and pithy phrase, the bit of apparently ordinary conversation, the utterance pared down to bone, even silence is often preferred as the most effective way to evoke and instill insight and wisdom in another. The short daggers with thin blades, the shafts of delicate light and zany remarks are like shorthand for the longer tale, the discourse. And the ground and backdrop of all the words and silence is the discipline of sitting—just sitting—and doing, thinking and being nothing. This is often referred to as meditation in the West. You can do it sitting like a lotus or walking; you can also do it raking sand into simple but intricate patterns, or washing dishes, or pruning trees or eating *soba* noodles loudly from a delicate ritual bowl. The meditation is the conscious living of daily tasks, the discipline of being just "here" and nowhere else, present to this moment and doing it with utter simplicity. Such meditation is called in Japanese *wabi-sabi*. It is hard to put into words, something like utter simple graciousness, expressed with as little as possible. In Western spiritual terms it might be kin to the virtue of poverty practiced as an art form.

Any saying, poem, *koan*, *haiku* (a seventeen syllable verse form of three lines of 5, 7 and 5 syllables) or story is as close as one can get to the physical presence or sense of the teacher long departed to the deeper realms of spirit and truth. All these forms are direct and to the point—a point that is finely honed and razor sharp and quick. They evoke laughter and are couched in an earthiness that can sometimes shock or scandalize Westerners. They are all part of the teaching process.

Their nature is playful, intriguing, annoying, outrageous, cryptic, infuriating, sobering, awareness-twisting. They deliberately throw our minds and souls a curve, or pull the rug out from underneath us and subvert all our previously held and cherished ideas.

And all involve a direct line of transmission, an experience that is immediately passed on and confirmed in both the individual and in the community that honors a particular tradition. It is interesting to note that one of the methods shared by both Jesus and Buddha (and others in the East) is the invitation to "Come and see for yourself." The teachings and discourse are vitally and radically connected to the person of the teacher. The writings are meant to produce an experience of enlightenment (*satori*) eventually, or a transformation of vision and life from within, or a conversion of the entire self.

This is especially noticeable in the *koan* or story. The sound of the story or saying or riddle is important. Sound and meaning are almost inseparable. Again, this understanding is shared by Christians and Jews. We hear it in Genesis when God speaks and the universe is set in motion, drawn forth from the void and arranged in order. And in Isaiah 55 the prophet, speaking with the voice of Yahweh, says:

> As the rain and the snow come down
> from the heavens and do not return
> till they have watered the earth,
> making it yield seed for the sower
> and food for others to eat,
> so is my word that goes forth out of my mouth:
> it will not return to me idle,
> but it shall accomplish my will,
> the purpose for which it has been sent.
>   (Isaiah 55:10-11)

God's word is creative. It literally gives birth. What is spoken is done, and it remains, echoing throughout the universe. Even if we don't hear or respond, it still retains its force and meaning and resounds wherever it is allowed to enter. Conversion, enlightenment, transformation presuppose a turning toward the sound, the intrinsic truth inherent in the words. Our lack of listening doesn't diminish the word's integrity or power. It is only we who remain lacking and asleep, locked inside our own fantasy, closed to reality. The power of the word uttered continues on in human beings. In Genesis we see Jacob, with help from his mother, "stealing" his older brother Esau's birthright. Prior to disguising himself so that his blind and aging father Isaac will think he is Esau the hunter, Jacob obtains permission from Esau and buys the blessing from him for a pot of stew. Jacob throws in some extra bread and lentils and something to drink (see Genesis 25:27-34). Then he goes to his father and obtains the first-born's blessing. When Esau comes in to receive the blessing he weeps aloud and plaintively asks Isaac: "Have you only one blessing? Father, bless me too." Isaac gives him this answer, "Your dwelling place shall be far away from the richness of the earth, away from the dew of heaven above. You shall live by your sword, and you shall serve your brother; but when you win your freedom you will throw off his yoke from your neck" (Gen 27:38-40).

It seems there is only one blessing and what has been put into words and spoken aloud stands as uttered. This applies throughout the testaments for blessings, curses and one's word of honor. Once given it is sacrosanct. If it is given unduly, or dishonestly, then one's very life is forfeit. We are our word of honor, our oath. It is, in some mysterious way, our true nature.

What does the transmission look like? There is a traditional tale that tells of how Buddha himself passed on his core insight and experience of enlightenment to his student, Mahakashyapa. It took place during one of the many teaching discourses Buddha held regularly as part of his disciples' training. The very title of the discourse helps one to remember this paradoxical story. It is called "The Sermon on the Mount of the Holy Vulture."

❋ Buddha was preaching to a gathering of his disciples. He sat upon the podium and remained completely silent for a long time, and instead of resorting to words in order to explain his point that day, he lifted a single lotus flower and held it in his hand for all to see. The disciples were baffled and could not understand the significance of his gesture, except for Mahakashyapa who quietly smiled at Buddha to show that he fully grasped the meaning of his gesture. Buddha, seeing his smile, declared, "I have the most precious treasure, spiritual and transcendental, which this moment I hand over to you, O venerable Mahakashyapa." Bodhidharma, who brought Zen Buddhism to China, was a direct spiritual descendant of Mahakashyapa. (*Sayings: The Wisdom of Zen*, p. 12)

This is just one example of a form of transmission, just one of the ways in which knowledge is handed over. It continues through a long line of generation that spans centuries and continents. And, through it, Buddha's voice is still alive in the world.

We are no longer able to hear Buddha's voice. However, we can still hear voices that come close to his. When all things of this world that have a voice together raise their voices, retaining their individual character yet combining them in one large sound, then we are very, very close to the sound of the Buddha's voice. (From the *Shoji Jisso-gi*, Japanese text)

The reality of this experience, this hearing and becoming, transcends culture, language, religions and continents. Many seek to discover their true nature by opening themselves to these techniques and experiences. And they have been translated into Western spirituality. In a piece of personal correspondence dated January 1966, the monk Thomas Merton writes:

Now you ask about my method of meditation...My prayer (rises) up out of the center of Nothing and Silence. If I am still present "myself" this I recognize as an obstacle. If He wills He can make the Nothingness into a total clarity. If He does not will, then the Nothingness seems (in) itself to be an object and remains an obstacle. Such is my ordinary way of prayer, or meditation. It is not "thinking about" anything but a direct seeking of the Face of the Invisible. Which cannot be found unless we become lost in Him who is Invisible.

The way is not always the way one expects, but it is the way. Another writer from the Far East puts it this way: "Our practice is to go against the flow, against the streams. And where are we going? To the source of the stream" (Ajahn Fuang). A Christian mystic says: "If a man wishes to be sure of the road he treads on, he must close his eyes and walk in the dark" (John of the Cross).

But the way is not always so "mystical" or obviously related to "the realm of the sacred or the holy." Anything can be useful for illuminating truth and reality. There is a tale told of a Zen master named Ikkyu (1394–1481) who was once chided by a magician for being unable to produce miracles. "On the contrary," Ikkyu responded, "in Zen everyday acts are miracles." Unimpressed, the magician performed an elaborate ritual and summoned up a fiery image of a fierce divinity. Then he challenged Ikkyu to perform an even mightier work. Ikkyu replied, "Here's a miracle issuing from my own body," and promptly relieved himself on the apparition, reducing it to a pile of soggy ashes (Stevens, pp. 32-33). In the Eastern tradition, everything is matter for teaching, absolutely everything.

Here are two parables from Japan that I heard while I was traveling and visiting monasteries there last year. This one is called "Iron Rods" or "Endurance."

✴ Once upon a time there was a young boy who, because his father had died, had been entrusted to the care of his uncle. Struck by his father's death, the boy became interested in Buddhism. He asked if he could join a temple and study, in hope of becoming a monk. The uncle set him up in a monastery and would occasionally visit him to see how he was doing.

The young boy was apprenticed to a monk of about seventeen who had been at the monastery for over a decade. He was the eldest son of a family who owned a large temple and he would one day be its head priest, following his ancestors before him. But he had grown indifferent and angry at his life in the temple and was short-tempered, ill-mannered and spiteful.

The uncle visited the master and was told that his nephew was doing well, very well in his studies, discipline and behavior. He was maturing and was obviously well-suited to the life of the monastery. The uncle left until his next visit, content that his charge was doing so well.

Winter came, and the monk that the boy served grew more and more irritated with the young boy's dedication and silent obedience. He knew that long ago he himself had given up such devotion, and the boy's presence made him aware of his own shallowness of practice. One afternoon, he ordered the boy to bring him a kettle and boil water for his tea. The boy brought the kettle quickly and hung it on the iron chain, over the coals. Then the monk yelled at the boy, who almost dropped the heavy iron kettle, losing some of the water and almost putting out the fire. Hanging on the wall by the fire there was a set of iron rods, like long chopsticks, which were used to stoke the fire. Without thinking, the monk grabbed one of the iron rods and hit the boy's bare arm with it, dealing him a severe blow just above the wrist. The boy tried to keep back his tears until he was dismissed and then ran into the bamboo grove where he could cry alone.

His uncle, who had come to visit that day, saw him crying and running away. He followed him and asked, "Why are you crying?" The boy said nothing. The uncle noticed the welt on his arm. "You are hurt!" Again, the boy said nothing. "Someone has hit you!" His uncle dragged him to the master monk and showed him the boy's arm, protesting that he was just a child and needed attention and care. What was being done to teach him and help him?

The monk arose, took a book off his shelf and handed it to the boy. He indicated a passage and asked the boy to read. The boy read aloud: "One who practices endurance will be a spiritual hero." The master ordered him to read it again, slowly, so that it could sink in. The boy obeyed. Then he was asked to read it yet again, even more slowly and with care.

The uncle sat watching and was furious. He grabbed the book from the boy's hand and shouted to the monk: "That's easy for you to say. It's easy to meditate on words of endurance when you're not hurting and haven't been struck without cause!" The master looked up at him and was silent.

After a long pause, he spoke and said: "You're right, of course. It is easier to meditate on the words when you haven't been hit and are hurting." With that, he went over to the fire, reached under his tea kettle, picked up one of the iron rods and dealt himself a severe blow. He returned the rod to its holder and went back to the boy. Handing him back the book, he said quietly and surely: "Let's read it together and meditate on the words: 'One who practices endurance will be a spiritual hero.'"

And another, that was told to me in Hiroshima on a night when the moon was full and shining over the bay.

* Once upon a time, Ryokan, the famous scholar and monk, decided to go into the mountains to live alone, meditating and praying. One night he stood by his kitchen window wondering what he would eat that night. He hadn't eaten in two or three days, so he was a bit concerned. As he stood there in the gathering dusk, the moon rose full in his kitchen window. It was glorious, full, white, a great silver coin shedding warm light everywhere. He was stunned by its beauty. In a moment he was out the door and chasing after the moon. He kept it before him, singing its praises and the praises of everything that was bathed in its light: the bare branched trees, the owl who brushed by him, the frozen puddles and roads. It was all

so lovely. Over the hills he ran, singing at the top of his lungs. Time seemed to stop until the cold began to creep deep into his bones and he knew that if he didn't go back to his small hut soon he'd freeze like the grasses under his sandaled feet.

Back he went, but the trip seemed longer and colder than the one out, when he had followed the moon. Finally he reached a rise and could see his hut on the next ridge. But then he stopped. There was a light burning in his small hut, like a beacon in the dark night. He thought to himself: I don't remember leaving a light on. No, it was dusk when I left to run out after the moonlight. Someone is in my house!

He covered the ground to his small hut quickly. Then he crept up and peered in the window. There was a thief in his house! The man was frantic. He was desperately searching through the small room to find something to steal and there was nothing of any value.

Ryokan burst into the hut and grabbed the man by the shoulders. "Sir," he exclaimed, "I can't have you leaving without anything of worth, especially after all your hard work in looking. Here, take my clothes and sell them!" With that, he stripped off his clothes and gave them to the stunned man, who grabbed them and ran out the door.

Ryokan was left alone, stark naked and shivering in the cold wind that came through his open door, along with the streaming moonlight. He went to the door and looked up at the moon. And he spoke softly aloud: "Ah, what I really wanted to give him was the moon!"

Now let us move to India, Iran, Turkey, Iraq, to the land of the Sufi, the teachers and *murshids* who claim one of the many mystical teachings of Islam. These stories and sayings are born of the desert, the dancing of the whirling dervishes, the poet Rumi and his disciples, Idries Shah with his tales of Nasrudin, and the oral wisdom born of the Koran, believed to have been dictated by the angel Gabriel to the Prophet. Reverence for the book, the words, the very characters of the text is instilled in the very young. "When a boy reaches the age of four years, four months and four days, [he] is dressed up like a little bridegroom and sent to school to recite his first verse of the Koran. The verse is written in honey on a slate and, after the boy masters it, the honey is dissolved in water. The boy drinks the sweet holy words as a spiritual and physical nourishment" (Goldman, p. 232).

Respect for the words of the Prophet extends to stories and tales about him as well as stories from the traditions of the wandering dervishes. Stories about Nasrudin are famous. Sometimes he is a wise man, at other times a fool, and then again, a trickster or prophet. You never know until you come to the end of the story and Nasrudin gets you, one way or the other.

* Once upon a time Nasrudin was eating his usual fare of chick peas and gruel and stale bread. He sat and ate slowly, chewing each piece thoroughly and making it last as long as he could. His neighbor, who lived across the street from him, dined daily on rich fare, brought straight from the king's own table and kitchen. One day, from his roof, he spied Nasrudin eating and called out to him: "My friend, what a pity you have such terrible food to eat. If only you would accommodate the king and tell him more of what he wants to hear, why then, you'd dine on rich food and drink like I do."

   Nasrudin continued eating and then called back: "If only you would learn to savor the taste of chick peas and gruel, than you would live in freedom from the king."

Nasrudin is blunt. He is unpretentious and prophetic in the ancient tradition of speaking the truth in season and out. But Nasrudin is an ordinary person struggling with his own inner weaknesses and faults too, like the rest of us.

* Once upon a time when Nasrudin was broke and wondering where his next meal would come from, as well as

how he would pay his many debts, he decided to pray. It was a banal sort of prayer: basic bribery. Oh Allah, most compassionate, you know my need. Please provide for me and I will give you a special portion of whatever you give. This I vow.

Well, no sooner had he finished his prayers than he spied at his feet an old coin. He snatched it up and continued on into the village with the coin in hand, already rethinking his vow. "Humm," he thought, "if only I'd waited just a few more steps, then I'd have had all the money to myself." He came into the village and went to a shopkeeper's stall. They bargained and argued. The man kept saying it was an old coin, not worth a new coin's value. He finally offered to give him 75 percent of the coin's value. Nasrudin had to settle for that, for it was better than nothing at all. As he left with his money, he remembered his vow, and his rethinking, his reneging on his promise to Allah. He smiled ruefully and prayed again: "Ah, how smart you are, Oh Holy One, to take your own portion right away, since I thought to deprive you of your share."

The teller asks: "I wonder, did Nasrudin keep the rest or give Allah his true portion, as he had vowed?"

Anthony De Mello in one of his talks tells a Sufi tale about Allah, whose first and primary name (out of one hundred names) is "the All-Merciful—the All-Compassionate."

✳ Once upon a time, a Sufi saint, on pilgrimage to Mecca, fulfilled all the practices required. He knelt down and touched his head to the ground and prayed: "Allah! I have only one desire now in my life. From this day forward grant me the grace to never offend you again, to never commit another sin."

It is said that when the "All-Merciful" heard this he laughed out loud and turned to one of his saints and said: "They all ask for the same thing. And if I granted their request, where would I be? I'd be left with no one to forgive and that would cause me great distress."

Another story begins:

* Once upon a time a beggar, really a holy dervish, came to the king with his begging bowl in hand, asking not just for an alms, but whether the king was great enough to fill his bowl. The king laughed and said, "Of course!" He summoned a servant and instructed him to fill the beggar's bowl with coins. He could be generous when he was in the mood and he intended to show this beggar what a great and wealthy king he was. The servant obeyed and filled the bowl with coins, more and more and more; hundreds, thousands—and still the bowl was nowhere near filled. The king became distressed, looking at the mouth of the bowl that was never full. He knew that if he kept trying, he'd end up poor himself: already he was feeling poor, helpless and foolish, caught out.

  He looked at the beggar with searching eyes. "Who are you? And what kind of bowl do you carry? You are making a beggar out of me. It is swallowing everything I own."

  The beggar looked back at the king and spoke: "My bowl will never be filled, no matter how much you put in it, for my bowl is the want that is found in the heart of human beings."

All the stories follow a pattern that is universal: they attempt to stop the listener cold. The stories help listeners reevaluate their priorities, gain insight into unconscious experiences of daily living, or reveal the mystery hidden in circumstances or events shadowed by pain, rejection and loss.

* Once upon a time there was a dog that decided to go see his friends in a distant town. The journey usually took three or four days, but this time the dog made the trip by sundown of the first day! His friends were surprised to see him. "It was a long journey, very hard, but I made such good time. I have to attribute it to the kindness of others, strange dogs I've never met before. Ever since I set out I've been moving at top speed. Whenever I stopped to

rest they'd be on me, nipping at my legs and growling and barking, so I had to keep moving or else get bitten. Everywhere I went it was the same, until I arrived here safe and sound, and so quickly. You never know when others will help you on your way!"

The Sufis share many techniques with Indian masters also intent on seeing mystery and the divine in everyday, even banal experiences. These experiences are ways of growing more intimate with God, often referred to as "the Beloved" or "the Friend." There is a desire for closeness, for the freedom born of poverty, for intensity in pursuit of the Holy. Often this pursuit is shared in a close company of followers of a particular master who teaches through poetry and stories. There is a sense that one is pursued, sought out, and trailed into every area of existence by the Beloved and that God does not let his children stray very far or be without him long. The sense of his absence is an even greater gift of the Beloved's care and attention.

One of the famous sayings of the Sufi is "The cloak of the dervish is submission. If you cannot bear injuries, you are but a pretender, unworthy of this cloak." The cloak of white wool worn by the Sufi is not only symbol of the search, but of the approach to the Holy, to the lover who intoxicates one in prayer, discussion, dancing and sheer need and desire for holiness. Dr. Nurbakhsh says: "Sufism is to walk towards God on God's feet." And yet this is always a balance between intense joy and just as strong sorrow. "What is Sufism? To feel joy in the heart at the coming of sorrow" (Rumi).

And the Sufi tell stories of Jesus, who is considered a powerful prophet, that sound a lot like Jesus' own parables. This one is called "The Highwayman Thief and the Elder Disciple."

✳   Once upon a time it is said that Jesus, son of Mary, was out walking, accompanied by one of the elders of Israel. As they walked and talked of eternal things they were met by a notorious robber, a thief who had plagued the country for decades. The thief saw that this was a holy teacher, probably with one of his favored disciples and thought, oh, to join them and become three. And even though he suspected that this man was a prophet of God and could read his soul, he approached them and fell in beside them.

The elder was engrossed in conversation with Jesus and for a few moments didn't notice that there was another with them. But when he did look up and notice him, he was angry that an obvious thief and brigand would attempt to walk with them. He instinctively moved aside, closer to Jesus, shutting out the man, so that he had to walk behind them. Meanwhile, in his heart, the thief was listening and thinking that perhaps he shouldn't have presumed that he could listen and draw near to someone so holy and truthful.

And Jesus spoke to both of them. "You must both begin anew, repent and be converted. From this moment on you are forgiven and all your past is gone, erased, as though it never happened." He turned to the thief and said: "Your evil deeds are forgotten because you were humble before us." And he turned to the elder and said, "And your good deeds are all gone because of your self-righteousness and disdain for your neighbor."

With that, the thief became Jesus' disciple and the elder left him.

It sounds a lot like Jesus' parable of the Pharisee and the publican. That stories jump traditions easily suggests that truth is not limited by such boundaries.

Another story clearly teaches Jesus' care for all who suffer unjustly and are poor, alone, innocent in their unnecessary pain—a value shared by the three Western monotheistic faiths.

✳ Once upon a time, it is said, Mary made Jesus a cloak, not the seamless garment that the soldiers cast lots for at his execution, but a patchwork cloak. It was as remarkable as Joseph's coat of many colors. It was truly the cloak of an itinerant fool, a storyteller or prophet. And Jesus wore it as he traveled and slept in it at night. When he ascended into heaven, this was the cloak he wore as he entered into his glory. Those who have visions of him always see him in *this* cloak, not a robe of glory, as some are quick to relate. In fact, one master, when he saw him, was pained to see his cloak grown faded and worn, full of rips, tears and resewn patches, even though beams of light shone from every patch.

He asked Jesus the Savior why he wore this cloak and why it was both so shabby and so full of light. Jesus answered, "These are the rays of my misery. Every rip and tear that I had to mend represents all the unnecessary sufferings and unjust treatment of the poor of the earth that have stung my heart. All of these I had to repair and God, my Father, filled them with light. I love this cloak more than any other." And so do all who follow in his footsteps. (A short, somewhat similar version is in Dr. Jarad Nurbakhsh, *Jesus in the Eyes of the Sufis*, Khaniqahi-Nimatyllahi Publications, New York/London, 1992, p. 92.)

The theme of God's compassion, the compassion we are to have with one another, is echoed in stories from the Christian tradition, such as Jesus' parable of the unforgiving debtor, or the unmerciful servant in Matthew 18:23-35. It is a simple story of a king who comes to settle accounts and finds that one of his servants owes him an enormous amount of money, money which could only have been stolen in business deals with the master's clients. The servant is about to be sold into slavery, along with his wife and children. Knowing he will lose everything, he begs for mercy. Not only is mercy given to him, but the debt is dropped altogether; it is wiped away and he is free.

He has no sooner known such mercy than he goes out of the master's presence and comes upon a fellow-servant who owes him a piddling amount. He throttles him and threatens him and the other man begs as he just did, but there is no mercy, no accommodation to allow the man time to repay him. He has him thrown into prison.

The other servants are badly shaken by the man's treacherous behavior, his lack of gratitude and sheer inconsiderateness. They tell the story to the king and the man is dragged back to be punished and pay the full price. Jesus' closing words are staggering: "So will my heavenly Father do with you unless each of you sincerely forgives his brothers." And forgiveness here is not a matter of mere words or psychological second tries; it applies to money, to debts and legal issues, to situations where there is actual indebtedness on the part of one party or another.

It is helpful to remember that Jesus teaches his disciples the "Our Father" when he is asked to show them how to pray. In the middle of the prayer is the line: "And forgive us our debts as we forgive those who are in debt to us." Scripture scholars like Eugene LaVerdiere point out that there are two words for debt in Hebrew and both of them are used in this sentence. The first indicates a debt that is unpayable, either because of its enormity or because of the nature of the relationship between the two parties. The second describes debts between equals, debts that are workable. The phrase then says, "Forgive us our unforgivable debt of sin and ingratitude as we forgive those who owe us little and have sinned against us." It is an expression of humility, of being sinners in debt to God. It is also an acknowledgment of the great mercy that is always extended to us by God, the All-Merciful, and of our response of grateful forgiveness extended to anyone who has wronged us or owes us.

Many of these stories are shocking, disturbing in content as well as in form. The thrust is to get inside us and stir up what is dormant and asleep, to help us refocus our lives on God and off of ourselves. But their underground currents are about hope, about humanity, about change and about newness. We end with a story, "The Water Carrier," written by a friend of mine, Christopher Witt, who has graciously shared it with me.

❋   He'd been a water carrier for a long, long time. For such a long time, in fact, that he could not even remember when he had first begun. It seemed as if he'd been at it all his life, as if he had been born to draw water from a spring and to carry it in a leaky wooden pail to those pilgrims who had come seeking to be healed but who were too pained from their wounds or too weary from their journey to finish the climb to the spring.

There are those who say that it is a sacred spring. They tell stories of a saint long dead, a holy man whose name has been long since forgotten, and of the miracles he performed. He touched people and healed them. He spoke and brought peace to those in anguish. Then one day he was gone. A tree grew by the spring, a dogwood whose bloodstained blossoms dropped into the water. No one could remember its being there before, and those who were given to fancy claimed it to be the spirit of the saint.

And ever since, people had traveled from all around to drink of the water from the spring.

Carrying his bucket, the water carrier climbed the familiar path that led through the gorge and past the grove to the spring. It was a rugged trail, steep, rocky and winding, and when he sat by the water he was exhausted. For years he had made that climb, though with the years the climb had tired him more. People were waiting for him, many people, more all the time.

They waited eagerly each day for the water carrier to appear. He would walk from person to person, ladling out a few drops of the precious liquid and talking. He would tell stories of the holy man, that great healer of long ago. Pausing now and then, he would retie a bandage or hold a child shaking with pain and fear. Whether it was the water, the stories, or the obvious love the water carrier had for his task and for each person he met—whatever the cause, people were healed. A few spoke of limbs that grew stronger, vision clearer, hearing sharper, though many noticed no improvement at all, and some were still to die. But each person left having been touched and feeling at peace.

Only once each day did he make the climb. Only one pail of water did he carry back down. And that battered wooden pail, its seams coming undone, leaked, so that by the time he reached the people hardly any water at all remained. He felt, at times, so useless carrying so precious a treasure in so poor a vessel.

Was it the climb that tired him so or the bucket he carried? Or was it the burden of looking each day into the eyes of those who came seeking to be healed? Their eyes were so filled with pain and with hope that if he looked too long he seemed to see his own soul.

Still exhausted, sitting by the spring, more tired than he could remember ever being, he thought of drinking the water. It had comforted others; perhaps it would strengthen him. But from somewhere deep within him—almost beyond consciousness—a memory awakened. It was a memory of long ago, of coming to the spring, and of being given the water to drink by another. It did not seem right to him to drink twice of the spring.

Instead, leaning back against the tree, he gazed deeply into the pool. He had heard stories of those who had lost themselves looking into the depths, but he had seen enough of pain and of hope not to be afraid. He seemed to see his very soul, and he was not alone. A light, a gentle haunting warmth drew him on. He could hear a voice, though it was more than a voice, for it enveloped him with an embrace. "Well done, good and faithful servant. Well done."

The water carrier never appeared that day. He was gone. Another tree grew by the spring, a weeping willow whose branches dipped into the water. No one could remember its being there before, and those who were given to fancy claimed it was the spirit of the water carrier.

Resources

Shemsu-'D-Din Ahmed, El Eflaki, *Legends of the Sufi, Selections from Menaqibu' L'Arifin* (Wheaton, IL: Theosophical Publishing House, 1977).

Mojdeh Bayat and Mohammad Ali Jamnia, *Tales from the Land of the Sufis* (Boston: Shambala, 1994).

Anthony De Mello, S.J., *One Minute Nonsense* and *More One Minute Nonsense* (Chicago: Loyola University Press, 1992 and 1993).

The Effendi and the Pregnant Pot, trans. Primerose Gigliesi and Robert Friend (Beijing: New World Press, 1982).

Ari Goldman, *Search for God at Harvard* (New York: Ballantine, 1992).

Inder Malik, *Fables of Wisdom* (Delhi, India: Raqhul Printers, 1987).

Manuela Dunn Mascetti, ed., *Sayings: The Wisdom of Zen*, part of a Zen Box (New York: Hyperion, 1996).

Anne Sinclair Mehdevi, *Persian Folk and Fairy Tales* (New York: Alfred Knopf, 1965).

Swami Prakashananda, *Don't Think of a Monkey and Other Stories My Guru Told Me* (Freemont, CA: Sarasvati Publishers, 1994).

Donald Richie, *Zen Inklines: Some Stories, Fables, Parables, Sermons, and Prints, with Notes and Commentaries* (New York: Weatherhill, 1982).

His Holiness Shantanand Saraswati, *The Man Who Wanted to Meet God* (Rockport, MA: Element Books, 1987).

Idries Shah, *Seeker After Truth* (London: Octagon Press, 1982).

John Stevens, *Three Zen Masters* (Tokyo: Kodansha, 1993).

7

Storytelling and Community

Native American, Latin American and African Traditions

———— ✳ ————

When you lose the rhythm of the drumbeat of God, you are lost from the peace and rhythm of life. (Cheyenne)

Listen or your tongue will become deaf. (Spanish proverb)

Until the lions have their historians, tales of hunting will always glorify the hunter. (African proverb)

It is said that Africa is the land of one thousand languages. With fifty-five countries (at the present time), the land is always changing: the boundary lines and the place names shift, some countries are still colonized, some are free, and some are just caught in a life-and-death struggle to survive famine, disease, drought and war. The languages are usually oral, though the major ones are now scripted and can be printed in Roman characters. The sounds, though, do not always translate well into those represented by the Roman alphabet and so there are additional symbols for certain sounds. For example, the click, which is part of many languages of the south, is designated by ! in the text. But in many countries it is the language of the conqueror that still dominates and prevails above indigenous tongues. The local languages are the tongues of the people, though the European languages are used for administration and government.

Much of the land is primarily savanna, or bush, a mixture of thorny bushes, trees and tall grass. It is difficult to farm or even walk through. There are large deserts and jungles and tropical forests, but these are not the norm. And Africa, contrary to popular belief, is not crowded, except in the area of the Nile valley and in large cities. Someone told me that the population of most countries is less than the population of Paris: in most countries the population is growing fast, but it is still relatively small, especially considering distance and land mass. And the people are still rooted in the land though they have had to deal with historical disruptions and invasions and, now, independence, technology, and the poverty which has resulted from the loss of resources brought on by colonization. The traditions link the people closely with sky, wind, water, earth, fire, with their ancestors and other spirits that dwell in these elements and are still active in the world, needing to be heeded. One is not alone, but part of a long vine that is wrapped around daily life and strongly rooted in the far distant pasts of beginnings. This is the continent where humans began and stories of beginnings still bleed into everyday life. And words, stories and music seep through all of life, interacting with earth's constitutive elements. Listen to this story from Ethiopia, in northeast Africa.

✳   Once upon a time, it was long, long ago when the earth was young, Fire, Water, Truth and Falsehood all lived together in a large hut. They knew each other well. Although they were polite and careful with each other, they stayed out of each other's way. Truth and Falsehood were usually on opposite sides of the room and Fire avoided Water's creeping fingers.

One day they all went hunting together and their hunting was exceptionally good. A whole herd of cattle! As they were leading the cattle back, Truth spoke: "Let's divide the cattle equally since we all worked together." They all agreed, except Falsehood who kept his thoughts to himself, planning how to get more.

As they walked along, Falsehood fell in next to Water. Falsehood whispered to Water: "Look, you and I are stronger than Fire and Truth. You take care of Fire. I'll handle Truth and we'll have lots more between just the two of us." It was decided. Water moved on Fire, putting it out in a great hiss of steam.

They continued on, with Water thinking about what to do with the extra cattle. And Falsehood walked next to Truth saying: "Look! Can you believe what Water has done to our warm-hearted and true friend? We must leave Water behind and take the cattle to high ground where we'll all be safe."

So they left the savanna and climbed into the foothills and up the mountain sides. Water stayed with them as long as possible, but had to give up. Water couldn't flow upwards. It tried, but slipped and slid down every time it tried to surge up the mountain rocks. (Look! You know it's true. Water always flows down mountainsides today.)

Just Truth and Falsehood arrived at the mountain top. Falsehood stood confronting Truth and screaming, "I am stronger than you. I am the master and you will be my servant." Truth faced Falsehood quietly and then said, "No, I will not be your servant, ever." They fought and fought but neither seemed to be able to subdue the other. Finally, exhausted, they called on the Wind to hear their complaint and decide who was stronger. Wind thought but didn't know how to answer. Wind decided to blow through the world and see what others thought about the matter. Some said, "One word from Falsehood, and Truth is destroyed." Others said, "No, Truth can stand against Falsehood even when words have been broken and bent." Some said, "Falsehood is often hidden and lives with everyone, and you never know when you will be tripped up. Look how easy it is to lie a little." Others countered, "Like a small spark in the dark, or the grass, Truth, even one person's truth, can change everything and bring it back home."

Wind was gone a long, long time, but returned to Truth and Falsehood. Wind spoke, "Falsehood, you are strong, it is true, but the fact is, you rule only in the absence of Truth, when Truth has stopped trying to be heard or to speak. This battle isn't over yet." (And so, it's been that way ever since. On which side do you build your hut?)

There is a saying both in Africa and here in the United States among African-Americans, as well as in Latin America, that puts this story into one line: "The shortest distance between human beings and the Truth is a story." One's words, the truth and life are all bound as one.

The following story has roots in Aesop's fables, but I have heard an African *griot* (storyteller) from Ghana give her version, in the Ashanti tradition and I have also heard it told in Nicaragua by an old grandmother. This story has a number of names: "The Lion's Advice," "Just Talking" and "A True Friend."

* Once there were two friends who had been inseparable from their youth. They did everything together, starting early in the morning when they finished their chores until late at night after the sun went home. They played and explored together, got into trouble together and stood up for each other with their families. They were like blood brothers.

One day they ventured farther into the jungle than usual and saw a lion approaching. They were both terrified and one jumped into the nearest tree, climbing as high and as fast as he could. The other cried out to his friend, "Help me, I can't climb!" But the other stayed put, at a safe distance. The one on the ground was frantic but remembered something he had heard from the elders when they returned from long trips away from home. Lions don't eat dead meat. He threw himself down on the ground, his heart racing, barely breathing and telling himself to be dead, because he was going to be if the lion thought he wasn't. The lion approached, sniffing and smelling. The boy forced himself not to twitch or move, praying every prayer he knew in absolute terror. The lion came closer, bent toward his neck, sniffed some more, and finally turned and walked away.

As the boy lay there on the ground he began to shake in tremors and could not stand up for a long time. His friend came down from the tree, pounded him on the back and congratulated him for his bravery and quick-thinking, telling him he couldn't wait to get back to the village and tell everyone the story that night. "Why," he said, "that lion was breathing down your neck, so close it looked like he was talking to you, whispering in your ear! And you didn't move."

The other boy answered, "As a matter of fact, he was talking to me. He was telling me to be more careful in choosing my friends. He was right!" And he looked at the other boy and turned his back on him and walked home alone, wiser and stronger, but with a scar in his heart.

Universal wisdom jumps oceans and speaks truthfully in a range of languages. And yet, each culture and nation and people has a truth to tell that defines them uniquely, that is a balance to another experience or way of living in the world. Bruce Chatwin, an English writer and traveler (1940–1989) tells of this experience someone recounted to him.

❋ A white explorer in Africa, anxious to press ahead with his journey, paid his porters for a series of forced marches. But when they were almost within reach of their destination, they set down their bundles and refused to budge. No amount of extra payment would convince any of them otherwise. They said they had to wait for their souls to catch up.

This sense of the visible and the invisible, of the realms of spirit and matter overlapping and influencing one another, is core to African, African-American, and Native American peoples. All are connected, all are related, all are tied together in a balance and harmony and all are affected by any action or word that can break the bond or strengthen it. There is a justice, a judgment involved in all of creation. And words are as strong as any deed. N. Scott Momaday tells an incredible story called "The Arrowmaker." It is not only a story of how to survive with cleverness and skill, but it is also a story about language itself. It was told to Momaday by his father and told so often he came to love it. He has no idea where it came from, other than his father's family.

*   Once upon a time there was a Kiowa and his wife alone in their tipi in the forest. It was night and they sat by the fire, with the tent flap open to the night. He sat making arrows. Good arrows have teeth marks on them, for a Kiowa always straightened the edges of the arrow with their teeth and then tried them in the bow to see if they were honed true. While they sat quietly, each working, the man sensed another outside the tent, close by. He began to speak to his wife quietly as though they were just talking of the day's events and things that husband and wife speak of when together. His voice was steady as he told her there was someone outside and not to be afraid.

    He took the arrow he was working on, chewed on it once more and put it in his bow, aiming to the right, the left, up above to see the angle and checking how straight it was. He continued speaking in his usual voice, "I know you are out there and if you are Kiowa you will understand me. I know you are there, because I feel your eyes on me. If you are friend, speak your name." There was no answer as he repeated his words again, aiming here and there, checking the arrow. And then he deliberately took aim and sent the arrow out the tent opening to the place where the enemy stood, pulled back on the bow and the arrow went straight to the enemy's heart. (Momaday, "The Arrowmaker," p. 21)

This simple story evokes many responses and questions, but for N. Scott Momaday, the Native American writer who gave voice to many young Native American writers in the last twenty years in the United States, it is a story about oral tradition and the life and endurance of a people. He writes:

> Heretofore the story of the arrowmaker has been the private possession of a very few, a tenuous link in that most ancient chain of language which we call the oral tradition: tenuous because the tradition itself is so; for as many times as the story has been told, it was always but one generation removed from extinction. But it was held dear, too, on that same account. That is to say, it has been neither more nor less durable than the human voice, and neither more nor less concerned to express the meaning of the human condition. And this brings us to the heart of the matter at hand: The story of the arrowmaker is also a link between language and literature. It is a remarkable act of the mind, a realization of words and the world that is altogether simple and direct, yet nonetheless rare and profound, and it illustrates more clearly than anything else in my own experience, at least, something of the essential character of the imagination—and in particular of that personification which in this instance emerges from it: the man made of words. (Momaday, "The Man Made of Words," pp. 49-62)

It is a fine story, whole, intricately beautiful and precisely realized. It is worth thinking about, for it yields something of value. We must be careful, however, not to impose too much of ourselves upon it. It is informed by an integrity that bears examination easily and well, and in the process it seems to appropriate our own reality and experience.

> It is significant that the story of the arrowmaker returns in a special way upon itself. It is about language, after all, and it is therefore part and parcel of

its own subject; virtually there is no difference between the telling and that which is told. The point of
the story lies, not so much in what the arrowmaker
does, but in what he says—and indeed that he says it.
The principal fact is that he speaks, and in so doing
he places his very life in the balance. (Momaday, "The
Arrowmaker," p. 22)

The man and the woman survive in this story through
speaking, through language, their own language. And they
live. Not only do they live, they live to tell the tale and pass it
from one generation to the next. In the telling is the salvation.
The oral tradition itself tells a story of the precariousness of
words, events and experiences. It conveys knowledge long before that knowledge has been recorded, whether on skins and
pictures or in the words of one's native tongue or a second
language. The story, like the people in it, lives.

Among the many Native American nations there are stories about where stories came from and the power of the spoken word. Here is an ancient poem called "Magic Words," an
anonymous Eskimo poem found in *Shaking the Pumpkin: Traditional Poetry of the Indian North Americans*. Note that "anonymous" often denotes an oral tradition that belongs to a tribe
or specific local community.

In the very earliest time,
when both people and animals lived on earth,
a person could become an animal if he wanted to
and an animal could become a human being.
Sometimes they were people
and sometimes animals
and there was no difference.
All spoke the same language.
That was the time when words were like magic.
The human mind had mysterious powers.
A word spoken by chance
might have strange consequences.
It would suddenly come alive
and what people wanted to happen could happen—

all you had to do was say it.
Nobody could explain this;
That's the way it was.

That's the way it was, and for many tribes and indigenous peoples that is still the way it is for those who can hear, who can listen and bridge the past and the present with words—the storytellers. They not only preserve and remember, they create or pass on gifts given to them. There are many tales of how stories came into the world, long versions and short, the most famous being "The Storyteller's Stone," told by the Seneca and other Iroquois nations, the peoples of the land from the Great Lakes to the east coast. It tells of a young boy out hunting.

✳ When tired, he climbs upon a great stone to rest and while he drifts in and out of sleep he is told a story, the first story. He is fascinated and so grateful that he leaves a gift, the squirrel he has just caught, for the stone and asks if he can come again. Initially he does not hear a reply, but he is so enchanted by the story that he comes back the next day as soon as he has hunted and places the animal on the stone, lies down alongside it and listens. Another story is given. And the next day another still.

At home he is scolded for not having any game and not contributing to the clan, but he begins to tell the stories he has been given. Eventually he tells them of the stone and the gifts he leaves behind in exchange for the stories. Every night he takes them to the beginning of time, tells them of truth and lies, of war and peace, of how things came to be the way they are and how to live, where to find medicine and what to do in hard times.

One day while he is sitting on the rock and being quiet after a story, he asks how to keep all the stories and not lose them. The great stone tells him he must find a stone for each story, put the stones in his game pouch and keep them. They will help him remember. Each time he takes out a stone he will know its story and he can keep them with him.

In some versions of the tale it is a young woman who tells him this after he has taken her to the rock and shared the Storytelling Stone with her. When she hears one of the stories, she tells him that she recognizes the voice: it is the voice of her grandfather and he always saved things, knowledge and events by collecting stones or reeds or sticks. They leave tobacco each time they hear a story. According to certain versions of the story the Stone spoke only in winter; when spring came and the pouch was full, the Stone went silent and did not speak again until the first frost. In most Native American communities the time of storytelling is the colder months when the community gathers to listen, to discuss and share the stories. Old and young come together so that all can know the wisdom of the earth and their ancestors.

There is an Abenaki story that I heard from Joe Bruchac that adds to this telling of the first tales. It is the story of a young girl.

＊ She listens to her grandmother and grandfather tell stories and wants to know where they come from. They laugh and tell her that the stories come from them. She says that's not what she means: "Where did they come from before?" And she is told that they come from the stones and that there have always been only a few who are patient enough to listen to the stones and learn their language. There are really only a few who hear the stories, collect them and pass them on to all the others.

She listens and thinks about this and knows it is now time for her to say something (that is how you show you are listening and have heard so the teller will know to go on). "But is that the whole story?" she asks. They look at each other and say, "No, there is more to it, because, you see, there are stories inside all of us and all around us."

It is a cold, cold night. They send her to the door of the house and tell her to stand outside for a moment and come back and tell them what she sees. She returns, shaking and rubbing her arms and dancing up and down and tells them that she saw the stars and the smoke from others' fires and her own breath like smoke in the air. They nod and remind her that this breath is born of the fire of life, that the stories, like our own breath, warm us and keep us alive. They say, "Sometimes you can see the stories better than other times, like when it's so cold your breath goes out visibly in the air. Just like breath, air, life, water, all the gifts the Great Spirit gave us, stories too to help us live and show us how to change. The stories are hiding everywhere in the world and sometimes inside us. We must work at listening to the wind, to our own breath and to others' words and then we will learn the stories."

The tale ends with the need to practice: practice listening to the wind, the air between the tellers and the listeners and our own breath of life. If we can sit in the silence and wait, the story will come and visit.

Stories for indigenous peoples are born with us, gifts given along with the rest of creation. They help us to see our responsibilities to all that share the world with us: animals, birds, two-leggeds, Mother Earth and Father Sky, the four directions and winds, the Thunder Beings, water, fire. For many Latin American tribes, like the Maya, stories came to us from the birds. Originally stories were told only in the language of birds; their music and harmonies were universal, given without thought to who overheard them, though only a few were quiet enough and open enough to hear. There is a story told of "The Boy Who Talked with Birds."

❋   Once upon a time there was a young boy who, with his father, worked every day in the fields, hoeing the corn and tending the earth around their small house. At noon when the sun was hottest they would sit under the same tree and eat their lunch of tortillas, beans and chipilin greens. They would sit quietly, content and at peace, for there was a bird that came every day to the tree and sang. After many days and weeks, the young boy noticed that the song was the same always. His father didn't seem to notice this. When the boy listened to the bird's song he would laugh delightedly. And then they would go back to work with a lighter heart.

One day the father asked his son what he had heard, what the bird was saying. "Oh, he just sings because he wants to, and I find myself laughing because I want to," he said. But the father wasn't satisfied with that answer. He insisted that the boy tell him more and, after several days of this, began to treat him badly. Without thinking, the boy told his father that the bird was saying, "One day your father will have to salute you." That angered the father even more, since it sounded like his son had lost respect for him and expected to be saluted by him. Soon the boy had to leave because his father turned so cruel. The boy wandered lost and bereft of all that he held dear.

One day he came to another place, where a great chief sent out a proclamation to all who would heed. It said, "Anyone who can interpret the loud crows' squawks outside my house will be given my daughter and inherit my kingdom." The chief was tired of being disturbed, for the crows came in the afternoon, in the heat of the day, when the chief wanted to rest. Many tried, but the crows kept coming. Each day they were louder and stayed longer.

The young man decided to accept the challenge and he approached the chief. He discovered that there were only two crows, huge black ribboned birds who squawked back and forth for hours. The chief said, "I don't want to kill them, but they are making it impossible for me to sleep or get any work done." That very day the young man sat up against the wall in the shade and listened when the crows arrived and began their loud cawing. He smiled after a while and told the chief this story: "The male crow says that the female crow abandoned her eggs and that he had to keep them warm until they hatched. And she squawks back that he didn't bring any food to the nest and she had to go off hunting for food. Now she's back to claim her children."

The chief crowed, "Ay, caramba! What now? Well, I think the male crow should take the young boy crow and the female take the young girl crow and raise them until they can see eye-to-eye." He looked at the birds and crowed and squawked and then spoke to them in his own language, just to make sure they understood. Off they flew and, since they didn't return, they must have been content with the judgment.

The chief was delighted and he kept his promise. There was a grand feast at which the chief's daughter married the young man. With time, she fell in love with him and with his stories and what he heard from the birds. Soon he inherited all that the old chief had owned. He gave a great feast and many came from faraway villages, for they all were bound to the great chief. He recognized two immediately: his parents who had grown older as he had. They saluted him, though they didn't recognize him. Bowing respectfully, they presented him with corn and greens and wished him health and long life with his family. The young man leaned down and lifted his father and mother to their feet. Surprised, they heard his voice and his words: "Don't you know me, Father? Remember the bird's song and the laughter and the words that one day you would salute me?"

The man asked forgiveness and wept. His mother wept for joy and they were embraced and taken into the boy's house. He told them, "One thing I learned from the birds was that we must learn to live in peace, because love can be reborn over time if we stay near to one another."

And so the story is told of the ones who understand the language of the birds and their songs still: they are the ones who make peace, heal, reconcile and bring families together again, making enemies into neighbors and kin. This is the way it happened. This is the way I was told and it is true, yes? (A longer, detailed version can be found in an old edition of *Parabola* magazine.)

Yes! Among all native peoples, storytellers are servants of the people, bound to remember the wisdom of the past and to hold the tribe together in the face of hardship, persecution, oppression, and hunger. Central to their telling of stories is healing and unity, preserving the identity of the tribe, the ties that hold them together and to the land itself. This story is universal. It has threads of the ancient story of Joseph dreaming of his brothers bowing down before him one day. It calls to mind the long journey to Egypt, his slavery and rejection and rise to power. When his brothers come to him for food in a time of famine, he recognizes them though they don't recognize him, thinking he is dead. He forgives his brothers and gathers his own family together once again, beginning the story of the nation that will wait for a leader who will give them a vision of unity and make them a people bound in covenant to God, with a future of hope (Gen 37–49).

This theme is shared by contemporary storytellers. Isabel Allende, who was born in Peru, raised in Chile, and is now living in the United States, is internationally known for her novels and tales: *House of the Spirits, The Stories of Eva Luna, Eva Luna,* and other books. In remarks at the American Library Association meeting in San Antonio she explained why she writes:

> I write to preserve memory. I write what should not be forgotten. I suppose all writers share this purpose: we want to keep a record of events, beliefs and relationships that shape us as individuals and ultimately as a society. Literature helps us understand how we came together as members of a family and a culture. It informs and comforts us; it can also shock and alarm us. But perhaps the most important role of literature is to inspire us. Books are the vehicles that can move us from ignorance to understanding, from indifference to compassion, from disdain to respect.

Books, stories, tales told conjure spirits and presences of the past, of those who have gone before and lived, struggling to be human and free. Allende concludes by saying:

> My dream is to see a world where gender, race, nationality, or class will not define or determine people's destinies, a world where tolerance and generosity will prevail. Literature and libraries contribute to make this dream possible.

What is true for books is equally true—if not truer—for stories told aloud in community. The highest aspirations and the most desperate hopes are hidden in tales told at night, when communities gather and encourage one another, especially at times when others seek to enslave and dehumanize them. Virginia Hamilton collects American Black folktales among many others. Her books help people to remember and offer African-Americans of today a rich cultural heritage based on stories from Africa and from the days of slavery and reconstruction. Her best known book is *The People Could Fly*, a collection of folktales. The last story, which is the source of the book's title, is definitely best saved until the end. (This is the way I tell it. A more formal version is in the book.)

✳   Once upon a time in Africa there were people who could fly, lots of people. They flew like "blackbirds over the fields. Black, shiny wings flapping against the blue up there." But then the ships came. Slavery. Exile. Sojourning in a foreign land. Families, whole tribes taken and put in the holds of ships. It was so crowded, there was no room for wings. Misery. Forgetfulness. The farther they got from the sweet smell of Africa, of food and land and freedom, the more they forgot about flying.

Some though remembered, and were careful. You couldn't tell from just looking who could fly. One old man was called Toby. And he worked in the fields with a young woman, call her Sarah, with her babe strung on her back. They worked. They slaved, for the Master. "He was a hard lump of clay. A hard, glinty coal. A hard rock pile, wouldn't be moved." He and his Overseer and Driver were always pushing the people on. Work harder. Move faster. Pick. Bend. If they didn't the whip cracked and their skin left them flying in the air. Sarah worked hard but the baby was hungry. Couldn't stop though. She'd get beat. The baby cried and Sarah, she was so tired, she couldn't sing or rock the baby while she hoed and dug. The Overseer screamed to keep that thing quiet. But it cried and the whip cracked over Sarah's back and the baby screamed, like any hurt child. They both fell, Sarah hurt more 'cause her baby was hurt. Toby helped them up.

Sarah knew how to fly. She'd been hiding it. She looked at Toby. Soon? Yes, soon it's time for you to go. You know how. But the whip came again, hard on Sarah's back and legs, tearing her dress. Toby stood between her and the whip, taking the blows. "Now, child. Go. Go the way you know how. Remember. Now, before it's too late. Use your strength." And he spoke, magic words that came out like prayers, sighs and murmurs, faster and faster, over and over again. She lifted one foot, awkward on air, then another and rose just above the heads of the others, clutching her babe, and began to fly. Higher still and then it came back to her: the memories, the air, the sweet life of freedom, Africa, home. She was lighthearted and free, like a bird. Off she went, over the fields of cotton, over fences and roads, over the big house and slave quarters, with the Master on his horse trying to catch her. But she was gone and they'd all seen it.

Next day was hot. One by one they fell, but they remembered. They'd heard the old man's words and they practiced them, over and over to themselves. They tried them out: rolling over and over until they got it right, springing up and falling down and up again and off. Toby would be there beside them, whispering and singing, sighing and praying and they rose, went away, free. Finally, the Master gave orders to get the old man, Toby, but he turned and laughed in the Master's face. "Don't you know," he said, "it ain't magic. It's us. We know how to fly. We free." And he started with the words again and they all straightened up, dropped their hoes and took each other's hands together in a circle. They started repeating the words, some say like "ring-singing" and they flew. They flew away to freedom, the ones that could and Toby was behind them, taking care of them. He was their seer and he could also see the ones who couldn't fly, the ones who couldn't leave. They were the ones he didn't have the time to teach the words to. They'd have to wait for their chance to run.

That night the Master said it was a trick, that it never happened. The man kept quiet in his fear. But the slaves that were left behind, they told the others, and their children and grandchildren. When they were free, they'd tell it again. "They did so love firelight and freedom and tellin'. They say that the children of the ones who could fly told their children. And now, me, I have told it to you." (Hamilton, *The People Could Fly*, pp. 166-173)

This is a tale of hope, of belief in spite of horror, a tale of imagination that cannot be touched no matter what is done to the flesh, a tale that makes us more human while revealing the side of human nature that is deadly and inhuman. These are words that save, that offer the food of dreams and a future to those starving in a world that kills and murders, enslaves and oppresses. Whether it is this story, or the long story of Exodus in the Bible, or the Native American tales of the Trail of Tears, all are tales told to keep memory alive, to take the pain and use it as fuel for the journey, to forge ties to ancestors and elders and the events of the past—moments of glory, of endurance, of life and of death. "All dreams spin out from the same web" (Hopi). And words are chains of hope stronger than or at least as strong as the chains of destruction.

There is story told in Cuba, but I've heard it in practically every country I've visited in Latin America and Europe. A version of the story by Ramon Guirao can be found in *Around the World Story Book* and in *The Best Meal and the Worst*.

✳ Once upon a time the Lord of the Universe decided to test the wisdom of one of his servants. He spent a long time deciding what the test would entail. He loved to eat, and so he finally decided on a meal. He summoned his servant who happened to be a ruler on the earth and ordered him to prepare the finest meal that he could think of for him to eat and enjoy with his friends. The servant knew exactly what to fix: his favorite meal, ox tongue.

When dinner was served, it was delicious, but the Lord of the Universe asked the cook: Why is this the best food?

He answered: What could be finer than the tongue? With the tongue you can tell stories, have great conversations, praise others, including you, my Lord, speak of courage and the ancestors and dreams to come.

The Lord was pleased, but he wasn't finished yet.

The next day he told his servant. You did well, but here's the next part of the test: make me a terrible meal, with the worst foods you can think of. Again, the servant knew exactly what to cook: ox tongue. The Lord ate, wondering why the same food was chosen, tasting it, chewing it and trying to remember if it was different from the last meal. Finally he asked the cook why he chose the same food for both meals.

He answered: What could be worse than a tongue? It can lie, slander, gossip, start a war, bite at another's happiness, insinuate trouble, destroy reputations, plant the seeds of distrust, and enrage whole nations.

Once again, the Lord was impressed by his servant's wisdom. He decided that this servant knew about power —about good and evil—and should be the Ruler of the peoples on the earth.

Vaclav Havel, the president of Czechoslovakia, reminded a Western audience in 1989 that any struggle for freedom and dignity must begin with the effort to reclaim and redeem the language, restoring true meanings to words corrupted by abusive regimes.

At the beginning of everything is the word. It is a miracle to which we owe the fact that we are human. But at the same time it is a pitfall and a test, a snare and a trial. More so, perhaps, than it might appear to you who have had enormous freedom of speech, and might therefore assume that words are not so important. They are. They are important everywhere. The same word can be humble at one moment and arrogant the next... It is not hard to demonstrate that all the main threats confronting the world today, from atomic war and ecological disaster to a catastrophic collapse of society and civilization...have hidden deep within them a single root cause: the imperceptible transformation of what was originally a humble message into an arrogant one...Having learned from all this, we should all fight together against arrogant words and keep a weather eye out for any insidious germs of arrogance in words that are seemingly humble. Obviously this is not just a linguistic task. Responsibility for and toward words is a task which is intrinsically ethical.

In this area, oral traditions and written traditions are one. Words can be dangerous and destructive, curative and encouraging, demeaning and insulting, nurturing and wise, or stupid and murderous. It is not just the content and meaning of the words; it is also their sound, their tone, and their placement with other words. We are responsible for the words we use, the stories we pass on, the tales that make us more human or less so, that repair breaches or tear apart relationships. Just as the world came forth in a word from the Holy, our words either create or kill. There are no neutral words or stories. There are words and stories that glorify evil, war, violence, hatred, nationalism, racism, oppression, injustice, or insensitivity toward the suffering of others; such words and stories must be shunned and exiled. There are stories worth telling over and over again and stories that should never be heard or put into the air, and it is in the telling that the difference is learned. In every storyteller there is a streak of the prophet who seeks to defend and be the voice of the ones forgotten, those who are weak, infirm, old, too young to speak or without access to the dominant forms of communication. The strongest stories are those that come from below, from underneath, from those who are considered foreign or strange or different.

There is a Cheyenne story that someone once gave me. It was written on a sheet of paper and copied and passed along to me in Oklahoma by a Cherokee woman, so I do not know its source. It's short and startling. It's called "How the World Will End."

✳   The earth is held up by a tall, tall tree trunk. This tree
trunk is like a sacred dance pole. The spirits of all living
creatures swirl around it in a beautiful rhythmic dance.
Great Beaver is slowly gnawing at the pole. When he is
displeased, he gnaws faster and the pole gets weaker.

We displease Great Beaver when we interfere with
the rhythm of the dance. Great Beaver knows and gnaws
faster and the pole tips a little. If Great Beaver gnaws
through the pole, the earth will fall.

That is why all creatures, especially people, must
keep the earth in balance.

So as not to anger Great Beaver.

A warning. A telling of an old truth. A story that catches
our modern way of looking at the world and history and relationships and puts them in simple terms that can be used to
alter our ways of being in the world. The story is a reminder
that we have to remember the ancient truths if we are all
going to live together and have a world to pass onto our children and our children's children.

The stories of indigenous peoples, Afro-Americans and
many in the Americas and around the world are intent on
keeping earth and sky, birds, fish, two-leggeds and four-
leggeds in harmony, caring for each other and working together so that all can live as the Creator meant us to live, in peace,
growing old like great trees left standing in old-growth forests.

To end, two very young stories that hopefully speak the
same truth, first about earth's creatures, and then about humankind. The first is called "A Secret of the Trees." It was the
first story I ever wrote, sitting up against a tree and watching
the trees opposite me, in a soft rain shower in western
Louisiana. I swear the trees told me the story and I wrote it on
a piece of scratch paper I had in my pocket, word for word as
it appears. I have never changed a thing, but knew I had to
honor the gift as given on that spring day more than twenty
years ago.

✳   Once, in the days following the very beginnings of all
things, there lived a tree. It was old as trees go—piney,

well-lined and scarred from time and heat and random blows from skies handing out rain and lightning touches.

Each year the tree made its meaning, ritually shedding its needles till a thick bed covered its feet and softened its stretching out into the space about it a few fingers at a time. It looked like all the other trees in the mild wood—except for one small thing. In the insides of the tree lived a fox.

Now, foxes usually live in hollow places in the ground. But when the tree was young it had been hit by another tree falling and had a good piece of its insides laid bare. It had taken years to cover over the hole and the tree had felt bad about its emptiness. It was always afraid of someday being cut off from the ground.

But the fox had discovered the hole one day and for some reason always returned to just that hole in that tree, and eventually he had moved in. He had been there so long that the tree had come to believe that it was natural for other creatures to live in one's hollow empty spaces.

More and more, with time, the tree wondered what the fox would do for a home when the tree fell due to the weakness of its internal structure. Before that came to pass, the tree decided it had to find a home for its houseguest the fox.

Now there was a tree that lived next door. It was a thin, fragile tree, that turned only light green in spring and nearly died each summer. It wasn't suited to housing anyone. It could hardly stand up by itself. But the trees had been close for years and one day the pine tree shared its concern over the fox's home with its thin friend.

Now the tree was thin, but it was young (as trees go) and it was still growing quickly. It hit upon an idea. Why don't I just shift a bit and start growing among your roots, right up alongside your old scar. It will strengthen your base, and still leave the fox a place to live in for a long time to come. And I might even live awhile longer myself, since I don't do too well alone when the seasons change and my thin covering begins to crack and tremble.

So, it was agreed. The young tree crept over and the old tree learned to accommodate its nearness to its insides, and the fox was happy too. In fact, all the other trees were so impressed at the strength and length of time the trees lasted together after that, that ever since then, if you walk in a forest—any forest—you will notice that all the roots run together and the trees fall over each other, living so closely that if one needs to bend or lean, there's another near enough to hold it up. And, if you listen, you'll hear in the silent woods the secret of the trees that stand against time: Leaning can make you live forever and your weakest places can be someone else's home.

Music and shared silence also create the sense of community, not only among the living but also across time and mortality with the dead whom we have loved. When a dear musician friend of Tony Cowan died, he wrote this story, "The Missing Music," as a way of joining story, music, history, the deceased, and those who are listening here and now.

❋   When the great composer Franz Schubert died, he was survived by a coterie of brilliant students who were fiercely jealous of each other and had competed for Schubert's favor. He was also survived by his brother, who knew very well how these musicians would fight for scraps of the deceased master's work. Schubert's brother gathered up all the music the composer had left behind and put it in a safe place. Then he took one of Schubert's last manuscripts and carefully cut it up into fragments, mailing one piece to each of the great man's students.

They were aghast, knowing that no copy of the original manuscript existed. Some of them decided to mount and frame their fragment, treating it with reverence as a kind of holy relic of the departed genius. But a few months later, Schubert's brother sent them each a letter suggesting that they overlook their rivalry and come together to perform this late work. After all, he wrote, wouldn't that be a greater show of piety and appreciation than merely holding on to the fragments as relics?

After much discussion and correspondence, Schubert's students agreed to come together and give a public performance of the work. The event was highly publicized and drew an enormous amount of enthusiasm from music lovers throughout the country. Only when the former students united was a copyist able to sort the fragments and produce enough versions so that all the musicians could perform the piece.

At the first rehearsal, however, Schubert's students realized that in the middle of the piece something was missing. More than just a few bars, it was a noticeable lacuna. Indeed, one of them had decided to withhold his fragment of the manuscript. When contacted, he abruptly refused to have anything to do with the project. He believed that his fragment would greatly increase in value because it would forever be known as "the missing music" from Schubert's works.

On the night of the concert, the musicians performed brilliantly and with deep feeling for the beloved composer. When they came to the part of the piece that was missing, they simply held thirty-two bars of silence, heads bowed, bows unmoving, and then continued to the conclusion of the piece. The audience was astounded by this silent acknowledgment of Schubert's absence, and many commented that it was the emotional climax of the evening. No one noticed the pianist who slunk out of the concert hall, his head lowered in shame, hiding a fragment of manuscript in his breast pocket.

Schubert's brother took the stage after the applause, addressing the assembly: "Tonight you have listened to one of Franz's final gifts to the world. The music we have heard has soothed us with the reminder of his subtle presence here. But it has also given us something more: there is no way to fill the hole in the world now that he has gone, there is no way to escape the silence, that rest which punctuated this performance. The quality of that silence, the remembrance of our own incompleteness, this is what compels us to come together again and again, so that the music will be completed by our common silence and there will, some day, be nothing missing. Only then will our collective work be fully performed."

Even though Schubert's students had shown such rivalry and animosity toward each other in the past, that night many of them embraced before they left the stage. They say the music of that night has often been repeated, but the silence has never sounded quite the same.

Who we are is only really who we are together, all of us. All the really true stories say that somehow.

Resources

Isabel Allende, "Excerpts from Remarks at the American Library Association Meeting in San Antonio, January 1996," in *The Hungry Mind Review* (Spring 1996)—a free paper in bookstores!

Kathleen Arnott, ed., *African Myths and Legends* (Oxford: Oxford University Press, 1970).

Joseph Bruchac, *Dog People, Native Dog Stories* (Golden, CO: Fulcrum Publishers, 1995) and *Four Ancestors: Stories, Songs, and Poems from Native North America* (Mahwah, NJ: BridgeWater Books, 1996).

Bernard Binlin Dadie, *The Black Cloth: A Collection of African Folktales* (Amherst, MA: University of Massachusetts Press, 1955).

Alma Gomez, Cherrie Moraga and Mariana Romo-Carmona, eds., *Cuentos: Stories by Latinas* (Brooklyn, NY: Kitchen Table/Women of Color Press, 1983).

Virginia Hamilton, *The People Could Fly: American Black Folktales* (New York: Knopf, 1985) and *Many Thousand Gone: African Americans From Slavery to Freedom* (New York: Knopf, 1993).

Vaclav Havel, *Open Letters: Selected Writings 1965-1990* (New York: Random House, 1992). When it was published, this book was cited by *The New York Times Book Review* as an exceptionally worthwhile book.

Danny Kaye, ed., *Around the World Story Book* (New York: Random House, 1960).

Tara McCarthy, *Multicultural Fables and Fairy Tales* (New York: Scholastic Professional Books, 1993).

N. Scott Momaday, "The Arrowmaker," *Parabola Magazine* (Fall 1995) and "The Man Made of Words," in *Indian Voices: The First Convocation of American Indian Scholars* (San Francisco: The Indian Historian Press, 1970).

Victor Montego, *The Bird Who Cleans the World and Other Mayan Fables* (Willimantic, CT: Curbstone Press, 1991).

John Mundahl, *Tales of Courage, Tales of Dreams: A Multicultural Reader* (Reading, MA: Addison-Wesley, 1993).

Americo Paredes, ed., *Folktales of Mexico* (Chicago: University of Chicago Press, 1970).

Michael Rosen, ed., *South & North, East & West: The Oxfam Book of Children's Stories* (Cambridge, MA: Candlewick Press, 1992).

Jerome Rothenberg, ed., *Shaking the Pumpkin: Traditional Poetry of the Indian North Americans* (Albuquerque: University of New Mexico Press, 1991).

Brian Swann, ed., *Coming to Light: Contemporary Translations of Native Literatures of North America* (New York: Random House, 1994).

Nancy Van Laan, *In a Circle Long Ago: A Treasury of Native Lore from North America* (New York: Knopf, 1995).

Richard and Judy Dockrey Young, eds., *African-American Folktales for Young Readers* (Little Rock, AR: August House Publishers, 1993).

8

Stories and the Mystical Tradition

————— ✳ —————

Never seek to tell thy love
Love that never told can be
For the gentle wind does move
Silently, invisibly. (William Blake)

Every sound I hear is Thine own voice.
Every form I see is Thine own form, My Lord.
(Pir-o-murshid Inayat Khan)

Every religious tradition has its mystics. Common to all of them is the difficulty, if not impossibility, of putting into words the experiences they have had of the divine. Mystical experience is the direct, or unmediated, contact with the Unnamable, the Ultimate, the Absolute. Words and ideas are inherently limited because they mediate between phenomenal reality (our experience of what is "out there" beyond our skin) and our inner world, or self. But such signs and symbols are NOT what is actually experienced! We always mediate our experiences to ourselves and others with familiar ideas, feelings, patterns and perceptions, but these descriptions are only approximations. What can the mystic tell us, then, when the Holy moves on her in a way that does not fit any of our generally adequate representations?

156

In the Christian tradition, the Book of Acts and the letters of Paul reveal that Paul had experiences of God that we would call mystical, such as, for example, when he was caught up in the Spirit and visited the "seventh heaven." One of the many stories of the Desert Fathers tells of a holy hermit who decided to teach. Everywhere he went, young disciples would quiz him on various points of faith and doctrine. Now, there was one young disciple who followed him closely but never asked him anything. Wondering about this, the good teacher asked the disciple, "Is there nothing you want to know from me? Why do you never ask questions?" The young disciple replied: "It is enough for me to be in your presence."

The scholar and mystic Thomas Aquinas spent his life writing his vast compendium of theology, all of which was predicated on the admission that God is ultimately Mystery. Toward the end of his life God gave him a mystical vision. This one mystical experience affected Thomas so deeply that he never wrote another word, and when one of his Dominican brothers asked him why, he reportedly dismissed his life's work as "only so much straw."

Nowadays, there is an entire area of Christian theology devoted to such mystical giants as Francis of Assisi, Catherine of Siena, Julian of Norwich, Hildegaard of Bingen, Teresa of Avila, John of the Cross, Meister Eckhardt, and others. Collectively, their lives tell the story of how God reaches us in such intimate ways that our only hope of expressing this contact is through art. John of the Cross wrote poetry; El Greco and William Blake painted; Hildegaard made music. We tell stories, and stories are a way of pointing beyond the obvious or familiar toward the ineffable, the sublime, the ecstatic, the place where God makes love to us in unspeakable intimacy.

The rest of this chapter consists of a new story entitled "The Cantor." Written by Tony Cowan, this story is intended to give the reader an opening into Mystery. For reasons that should now be clear, no explanation or analysis is added. May you be open to allowing the story to take you where it will.

❋ In the center of the island of Atlantis lay the heart of civilization, the Temple of Sitnalta. Over generations, the people of Atlantis came to view science and technology as more relevant to their lives than religion, and their Temple activities were relegated to the status of moral entertainment. Despite its obsolescence, the Temple retained its rituals and traditions and protected its finest asset, the choir. One rule had never been challenged: the Templemaster, who was also the leader of Atlantis, had to be chosen from the ranks of the supreme cantors who not only led the choir but presided over the major rites. During this period of religious decline, a child was born who would reverse the trend of power and alter the history of Atlantis. This is his story, the story of Emdlen, the cantor.

It was a defining moment in the annals of Atlantis when the island leader resigned as Templemaster to rule solely as a secular governor. He had done this in order to create two distinct orders of society. Thus, he ushered in a new era defining religion as a sphere that stood to lose its integrity if used for political and social control. Seen as both pragmatic and enlightened, he became the most popular leader in Atlantean history.

He had a son, Emdlen. Because of his father's position, Emdlen grew up surrounded by wealth and privilege. His father expected him to succeed him as governor. By the time Emdlen reached the age of twenty, he was a brash, flamboyant socialite, precocious and talented. His greatest gift was his voice. Whenever he spoke in public, people said he would make a superb orator. Whenever he sang, people said he could become the first singing governor, a new breed of artist-leader.

One day, however, Emdlen went to hear the choir at the Temple and his life changed. The building was filled with people who had come for the annual Creation of the Earth ritual. When the music began, a preternatural presence took hold of the people's spirits and they swirled together in ecstasy. Emdlen had never experienced his soul nor a communion like this. The following day, he went to speak to his father's religious successor, the Templemaster Ehrgair.

"I want to be a cantor here in the Temple!" he announced. "Listen to my voice and you'll hear why." Emdlen sang and the Templemaster listened with closed eyes. Glorious baritone sonorities reverberated around the courtyard. Ehrgair said nothing for a long time.

"Like your father, you have a sweet voice, a voice that draws attention to itself. You sing with consistent tone and clarity, never wavering. I cannot possibly allow you to be a Temple cantor."

Emdlen lost his smile. "What? How can you possibly refuse? I have a great voice! My father is the governor! Why can't I be a cantor? I can do anything I want in Atlantis!"

The Templemaster was deliberate: "As your father well knows, if you were to sing in the Temple, people would listen to you and would enjoy your voice. This is not the purpose of the cantor. The cantor is one who disappears while the people's spirits are lifted together into a higher world. You would merely entertain them, stifling the ritual with your amazing show of talent."

Emdlen trembled with anger as he absorbed the finality of the words. He was still determined. "What do I need to do to gain access to the rank of cantors? I'm smart and I can learn anything."

Ehrgair responded: "When you can answer these three questions, you will be ready to assume the role of principal cantor in the temple. First, what is the sound the earth is making? Second, what is the sound God is making? Third, what is the sound you are making?"

Emdlen repeated the questions and strode to the doorway. He looked back at the old Templemaster and grinned, delighted with this unexpected challenge. Ehrgair bowed and said: "I will await your answers. Take your time."

When the young man told his father about his new-found vocation and his determination to follow it, his father was reluctant to see his son go back to the religious milieu he had left. Eventually, however, he agreed and told Emdlen to enroll in the Temple choir school at once.

True to his word, Emdlen proved to be a brilliant student and surpassed his tutors' expectations. No other chorister could equal him in tone quality, enunciation of difficult texts, or vocal range. In just three years, he had completed the entire seven-year course of studies and had passed all the examinations with distinction. He had even memorized the entire library of Atlantean spirit-lore, eleven volumes of intricate and arcane lyrics.

Returning to the Templemaster, Emdlen made his request again, but this time he sang it, improvising and loading his phrases with longing. He looked Ehrgair in the eye. Ehrgair nodded. "What is the sound the earth is making? What is the sound God is making? What is the sound you are making?"

Emdlen was crestfallen. He had long ago dismissed these questions and thought his musical discipline would be enough to convince the Templemaster. The Templemaster was as firm as ever.

"Young man, your raw talent is now cooked. But it is still unfit for the Temple. You must season it with the answers to these questions. Do not spend another three years ignoring them. Everything you need to know you could learn right here in Atlantis, but I suspect you would profit more by traveling the world to learn the answers at their sources. Talk to your father and see if he does not agree with his old friend Ehrgair."

Emdlen retreated to the governor's palace and lowered his head when his father laughed at the outcome. "Then you shall set sail, my boy! You shall go on a quest and the world and God will teach you all you need to know." Emdlen searched his father's radiant face, seeking knowledge that seemed just beyond his reach, wondering if his father was in collusion with the Templemaster. Ten days later, Emdlen sailed from Atlantis.

During the voyage, Emdlen's crew taught him to pay attention to the chorus of the ocean, the wind, the sails, and the groaning of the ship's lumber. Emdlen quickly tired of seafaring. Soon his voice could be heard emanating from the bowels of the ship as he practiced scales and arpeggios. The ship reached Australia and Emdlen set off alone, not really caring whether it was safe or wise to do so.

For months he wandered, concentrating on the sounds of animals, birds, and the elements. As his ears became more sensitive, he found he was able to hear insects and worms writhing under the ground and inside the trunks of trees. He had to cover his ears during thunderclaps and his sleep could be broken even by a change in the pitch of the wind. At night, he became conscious of the noises of his own heartbeat, breathing, and digestion. He learned that by sitting still for long periods in the evening, certain animals would draw near to investigate; when he synchronized his breathing with theirs, they would sing him dulcimer songs of wildness. This was how he learned the meaning of the wolf song. It had never occurred to him that wolves could hear the daytime roar of the sun's ignition and the shining of the moon as it lit up the night. The wolves were harmonizing with the planets. Thus attuned, Emdlen learned the answer to the first question.

One night, after attending for hours to the voices of a waterfall, Emdlen waded in and knelt beneath the downpour. The timbre of the falls filled his ears while the waves percussed his reed-like body. The chaotic earth tones he was now used to hearing receded. Beneath the cyclical noise he heard a steady moan, a huge vibration that resonated within him, not in his ears or head but near the base of his spine, deep in the roots of his body. This subterranean wave moved erratically within the globe of the earth back and forth between the thirty-six points on the surface of the planet. Like the sun and the moon, the earth was generating its own internal music. Now this music had become a part of Emdlen.

When he regained consciousness, Emdlen found himself washed onto the riverbank a short distance from the falls. A group of Aboriginal women had gathered around him, fascinated. Seeing his condition, they picked him up and carried him to their village.

Communication with the Aborigines was difficult at first, involving a lot of gesticulation and drawing on the ground. Then the village dreamkeeper arrived. She was an ancient blind woman to whom everyone deferred. She sat down in front of Emdlen and laid her palms over her eyes. He closed his. Within seconds they entered a trance state in which Emdlen was able to explain his quest and ask her for help. She understood more than he had thought possible. Better yet, she agreed to help him.

After six days of eating, sleeping, and recovering from his wanderings, which the Aborigines referred to as *tjukurpa* or "dreamtime," Emdlen sat under a tree to meditate on the second question. He was startled by an urgent tapping on his hand. It was Kunmanara, the dreamkeeper. She motioned to him to follow and glanced around as if she were checking to make sure they had not been seen. They scurried off and Kunmanara led him a long way from the village. Her blindness did not noticeably slow her movements. She brought him to a bush in which she had hidden a long, hollow tree limb and gestured for him to sit. Emdlen felt both curious and nervous as she stood lifting the wooden limb until the end of it was inches from his forehead. As soon as she breathed into it, sounding its peculiar tones, Emdlen had to close his eyes. Something between and behind his eyebrows was gyrating. The pitch of the notes was neither high nor low, yet it remained impossible to locate. At first, Emdlen listened to Kunmanara's breath becoming vibration, then he listened to the fluctuation in volume, and eventually he noticed the extremely high and low harmonics that were sounding with the fundamental tones. Led by these harmonics, Emdlen came face-to-face with their sources.

"I am Sandalphon, Harmonizer of Worlds, Sandalphon, Conductor of the Absolute Sound, Sandalphon, Cantor of the Infinite Sublime." The being that confronted Emdlen was towering and brilliant. The spirit's voice contained all sound, all frequencies, and induced the sensation of being sung to by vast choirs. Emdlen could not speak, nor could he take his eyes off the immense archangelic presence before him. At the word "cantor" he trembled.

The spirit continued: "I am evoked to guide you to the sound of the Supreme Being. You cannot hear or understand it yet. You must cross ocean and mountain, to Tibet. There the master musician, Huthaum Re of the Bon, will teach you to become silence. Only in total silence is the true sound. Only in total hearing is harmony, pure harmony."

Emdlen opened his eyes and found himself lying in a deserted place. Kunmanara was gone. He journeyed back to the ship and, with the voice of Sandalphon ringing in his ears, immediately commanded the crew to set sail for India.

Twice on the voyage severe storms threatened the ship, but Emdlen calmed them by intoning the sound of the earth. This overrode the random vibrations of the weather with an intensely focused larger harmonic pattern. Some of the sailors felt the strange, irresistible reverberation in their loins and along the cables of the ship, but none could tell where it was coming from. Certainly none of them would have thought it had a human origin. They were just grateful that the storms dissipated.

Emdlen realized that he no longer craved the admiration of the sailors and had lost his need to impress them. The sense of the sacredness of what he had already learned and the awesome revelation of Sandalphon had dislodged his arrogance, pushing him beyond superficiality. He knew instinctively that he must cloak his new power rather than advertise it, so he kept up his former habit of singing and practicing below decks. Some of the crew wondered whether he had learned anything valuable in Australia; they had to admit, though, that the rigors of seafaring were seasoning him. They liked to see him climb the rigging at sunset to take in the dusk; little did they know he was listening to the crescendo of the stars.

After docking in the Bay of Bengal, Emdlen and six companions made a grueling trek across the harsh terrain of India and the mountainous expanses of Nepal. After eight months, they reached the Bon monastery in Tesmon, Tibet. Huthaum Re was expecting Emdlen. This mystified his Atlantean companions, but they were so relieved to find welcome and shelter that they asked no questions when Emdlen and the whispering monk went off together.

Huthaum Re was an exotic sight even for a cosmopolitan Atlantean. He was a loftily erect man with disproportionately small hands and a leathery neck. His eyes were heavily lidded and his bald head had a mottled look. He moved with ritual grace, speaking only in a whisper, and his smile revealed bright yellow teeth and receding purple gums. His clothing seemed too flimsy for the Tibetan climate, consisting of one long robe of yak's wool dyed all the colors of the spectrum.

When they were alone, Emdlen found that Huthaum Re could communicate with him mentally the same way Kunmanara had, and he also understood perfectly Emdlen's Atlantean speech. Soon after they had spent their first day chanting and toning together in the Habdran Cave near the monastery, Emdlen felt compelled to ask: "Master Re, why do you never speak with a clear voice? When you are not sending your thoughts into my head, you only whisper. Are you afraid to cause an avalanche?"

Huthaum Re chuckled. "I will tell you why I whisper. When I was just a young *bonpo*, I entrusted myself to an old monk who was a *grubthob*, that is, someone with special powers. He initiated me into the mysteries of sound."

"Did he also whisper like this?" Emdlen interjected.

"Oh yes! Oh yes, he did!" Huthaum Re giggled. Abruptly he closed his eyes and leaned back, chanting ancient mantras:

"Sound creates shapes and beings.
Every atom dances.
Everyone and everything ceaselessly sings itself.

The *dorje* and the bell,
The *gchang* and the *gzungs*,
Singing bowls and *tingshaws*, ring *gyatams* down!"

So mesmerizing was the monk's chanting that Emdlen was instantly entrained with his thoughts, movements and sounds. They chanted in unison for hours:

"Sound creates shapes and beings.
Every atom dances.
Everyone and everything ceaselessly sings itself..."

Huthaum Re stopped as suddenly as he had begun. "I have taught you all you need to know." He jumped up and strode toward the mouth of the cave. Startled and dismayed, Emdlen shouted, "What? No! Wait! I didn't get..." There was a deep rumbling noise above and behind them. The ground shook. Within seconds a wall of snow had fallen across the entrance to the cave, sealing both Emdlen and Huthaum Re in darkness. For a long moment, neither said anything.

"I whisper because if I were to use the full force of my voice things would be created and destroyed all the time. Just as you were entrained by my chanting the mysteries, both earth and spirit are entrained by the energy and vibration of intentional sound. My voice is entrained with the humming of the Supreme Being. But beware: the power to create with sound is also the power to destroy, and a little coherent wave will penetrate infinite chaos."

Emdlen sat for a long time, then bluntly asked, "How?"

"If Sandalphon had not commanded it, I would never have told you. That will take a deeper cave. Tomorrow, perhaps. We have to get out of here now. Take this as a demonstration and a warning." With that, the monk spoke aloud, giving each syllable a whole breath, "*Nei noy rahm nei keeng!*"

The snow banked up across the mouth of the cave evaporated into wisps of steam. Blinking in the returning sunlight, Emdlen took the monk's hand as Huthaum Re helped him to his feet and smiled at him. As they walked back to the monastery, Emdlen glanced down at another snowbank and mischievously muttered at it *"Nei noy rahm nei keeng!"*

Nothing happened. Huthaum Re shot him an amused yet admonitory glance. "No entrainment, no knowledge, no power," he whispered.

After four months of intensive lessons, Huthaum Re woke Emdlen shortly after dawn one morning by speaking his name aloud. Emdlen washed, dressed and went to find the monk waiting outside the monastery gate. Without a word, Emdlen followed him on an arduous hike through the mountains until they entered a cave unfamiliar to Emdlen, much deeper than the Habdran Cave.

"This cave is special to Sandalphon," was Huthaum Re's only explanation. Emdlen followed the monk into the darkness of the cave, holding onto the back of his robe for guidance. For a long while it was pitch dark and Emdlen wondered how large the passageway was. Then unexpectedly, Emdlen's feet fell on rock and there was an echo. They had emerged into a cavern. The monk stopped and waited for Emdlen to catch his breath.

"Now, Emdlen, this is where you will learn entrainment. You will tune your ears, heart, mind, and voice to the sound God is making. This is where I learned the mysteries long ago." The monk paused: "Dark, isn't it?"

"Totally!" Emdlen agreed.

"Only in total darkness is the true light," Huthaum Re began, "Only in total silence is the true sound. Only in total hearing is the true voice. Emdlen! Become wholly silence!"

Momentarily, Emdlen was frightened by the monk's intensity, but he obediently poured his ears, heart, and mind into the silent immensity of the cavern. He heard their breathing, their heartbeats, blood circulating, muscles twitching, even nerve fibers firing. Then all at once he plunged into total silence.

Huthaum Re sent the thought command to him, "It is dark. Make it light!"

Emdlen felt a single note issue from his heart. It shot into his throat and then into the center of his brain. Opening his mouth he toned a syllable inaudible to human ears and suddenly the cavern was filled with a pulsating, yellow luminosity. His sound had created light! He stood there awestruck, repeating the syllable as the light grew stronger. Looking at Huthaum Re he saw they both had tears of joy in their eyes.

Before Emdlen and his companions left the monastery to make the long journey back to their ship, Huthaum Re took him aside and kissed him on the forehead, the throat, and the chest. His whisper was uncharacteristically constricted with emotion, "Remember, Emdlen: the sound God is making is that total sound found only in absolute silence. When you use it, as you assuredly will some day, make sure your own sound is coherent with it, or there will be destruction, not creation."

These words haunted Emdlen on the journey back to the Bay of Bengal as he wondered how he could possibly discover the answer to the third question. What, after all, was the sound he himself was making? Not even Huthaum Re had been able to tell him that.

When the crew was reunited, most were excited and curious to know what had happened during the intervening months. Emdlen told them he had taken singing lessons from an old master in the caves of Tibet. He was deliberately obscure in reply to further questions. The crew had evidently been building up hope that on his return they would sail back to Atlantis. Apologetically, he explained that there was something more he still had to learn. He announced he would attempt to learn it right there in the forests of eastern India and then they could sail home. He asked them to give him another nine months. When the majority agreed, he decided, despite his six companions' protests, that he would set off alone to penetrate the forests and jungles. When a crew member suggested he take a weapon to protect himself against predators, he answered firmly, "I speak their language.

That's all the protection I need." Finally, Emdlen had to agree that if he did not return within nine months, they should set sail without him.

Emdlen wandered endlessly through forest and jungle. He crooned with the hyenas and wolves and sang with the birds. But whenever he found a place to lie down and rest, he realized how lonely and vulnerable he was. For the first time since leaving Atlantis, he questioned what he was doing. In his dreams, he remembered how easy and safe his life had been in the house of the governor. He dreamed of his father staring out to sea and worrying. He had nightmares in which the Templemaster Ehrgair changed the strict rules of the Temple to allow anyone with a good voice to become a cantor. He wept when he recalled the beautiful communion he had shared with his fellow citizens at the Creation of the Earth ritual on that fateful night. He realized how shallow his studies had been at the choir school, where he had been driven by his desire to stand out. Picturing himself returning to Atlantis to share what he had learned, he could not bear the thought of merely performing and putting on a show. He regretting having used his voice so often to manipulate and seduce. He no longer saw himself as an aspiring artist. He would be a cantor. But he no longer knew clearly what this meant.

After weeks of wandering, and after many sleepless nights and several days without food, Emdlen found himself in a feverish state. He was searching for fresh water. In addition, he was obsessing over the notion that if he returned to Atlantis with only the first two questions answered, maybe that would satisfy Ehrgair. Yet doubt drove him deeper into the forest.

Exhausted and sick, Emdlen fell to the ground. Lying still, he listened for a waterfall or a river. Before he heard the river, however, he heard a sound so familiar yet so strange that for a moment he did not know what it was. Someone nearby was singing. Emdlen dragged himself toward the sound and peered though some bushes. There was a human being bathing in the river and singing. Was it a man or a woman? The voice alternated easily between soprano and baritone notes so it was hard to tell. The face was beautiful and swarthy, wild; the hair long and black. Emdlen's vision was blurred from lack of nourishment, but his ears were as sharp as ever. He fell in love with the singer's voice and took delight in discovering another human being in this lonely place. "A cantor, at that!" he rejoiced.

But when Emdlen waved to the singer and called out, tripping through the bushes near the riverbank, the singer cried in fear and dove underwater, swimming downstream. Emdlen tore his clothes off and dove into the river in pursuit. This was a mistake. He soon found himself so weak and exhausted from the exertion and the currents of the water that he began to drown. He breathed in water. He lost consciousness.

The next thing he knew, Emdlen was coughing and gasping for air. He felt someone's hands on him, someone bending over him and rhythmically pounding his chest. There was a searing pain in his heart and lungs. Opening his eyes, he blinked back tears and looked into the face of the singer. Warm, concerned and frightened brown eyes looked back at him. For the first time in his life, Emdlen felt alive and in love.

"You saved my life!" he croaked, wrapping his arms around the singer. The singer held him and then kissed him tenderly, crying along with him. Emdlen pulled the singer's body tight against his own and started to speak in a tone intended to comfort them both, "My name is Emdlen. I meant you no harm. I just heard your voice and I..." Without waiting for him to finish, the singer watched Emdlen's mouth moving and then put one hand over it to stop him from speaking. The singer's head was shaking as if to say no. The singer covered both ears and looked at Emdlen as if to say, "You understand?" Emdlen suddenly understood. The singer could not hear his voice. The singer was deaf.

During the time they remained in the Indian forest, the singer and Emdlen fell more deeply in love. The more they fell in love, the more they were able to communicate using thought alone. They learned much about each other. The singer had been abandoned by family and tribe because of the disability and psychic powers that had been manifested in childhood. The singer lived a wild existence among the animals and spirits of the forest. Emdlen was at pains to explain the larger world he knew, and his friend seemed to understand best through directly received images and intuitions.

One day, as they sat together by the river where they had met, Emdlen suddenly realized that several days had passed and he had not used his voice. Surprised, he cleared his throat. Then it dawned on him that the singer truly loved him without even being aware of his greatest gift, the one thing Emdlen had always relied on in gaining the esteem and affection of others: the sound of his voice. Emdlen's lover turned to touch him and found him sobbing, rocking back and forth with his knees drawn up to his chest, trying to send garbled thoughts of amazement, joy, freedom and gratitude.

The first half of the voyage back to Atlantis went well. The crew was happy to be returning home after their three-year odyssey. Emdlen now lived for something wider and deeper than his youthful ambition. The cantor and his beloved from the forest would settle down to a life together on the island and Emdlen would teach at the choir school. Emdlen was bitterly disappointed that he had not learned the answer to the third question, yet he consoled himself with his lover's blithe singing. At least he knew the sound his soulmate was making!

One day, as Emdlen was intoning the exercises he had learned from Huthaum Re, his lover came to sit with him. Emdlen brought his mouth close to his friend's forehead and began to tone the sounds of earth and spirit. What happened next neither of them expected.

The singer was raised, body and soul, into a higher world, a world which co-exists with this one but is both truer and more beautiful. On this plane of higher vibration, for the first time the singer was able to hear. Emdlen's beloved heard first the sound the earth was making; second the sound God was making; and finally, the sound which Emdlen was making! Now it was Emdlen's turn to open his eyes and be surprised to find his friend weeping for joy. After that, Emdlen delighted in bringing such moments of ecstasy to his lover often. His lover regretted being unable to duplicate the sound Emdlen was making in the "inner upper world." For Emdlen, it was enough that his soulmate had heard it.

The second half of the voyage veered away from joy. Emdlen's lover fell sick with a fever. The ship's doctor was unable to help because the cause of the illness could not be determined. Emdlen stayed constantly by his lover's bedside, unable to eat or sleep. He tried toning many times but to no avail. The singer remained delirious. Emdlen was despairing. To see the body of his lover writhing in torment was greater anguish than his own loss of happiness and companionship.

Without warning, a gale-force storm descended upon the ship. So heartsick was Emdlen that he did not even realize the ship was in danger until a crew member ran into his cabin and begged him to help, as all hands were needed.

Startled to hear that the lives of the entire crew were in jeopardy, Emdlen forced himself to leave his friend's side. He clambered up onto the prow of the ship where he lashed himself to a brace and began with all his remaining strength to go inside, to become still and silent, to let the wind and the waves crash over and around him. With one extreme surge of determination, he unleashed the sound the earth is making into the heart of the thunderheads above them. At first, the winds and rain were not assuaged, but gradually, as he reached down to the base of his spine and repeated the sound between gulps of salty wet air, the storm began to disperse. The clouds lifted and parted as if being blown away with his breath, the ocean stopped roiling, and the wind subsided.

As crew members scrambled to help the injured and account for all personnel, Emdlen collapsed. At that moment, he saw his soulmate fade away from him into a darkness like deep ocean or night sky, a vision of sorrow and joy, and before his lover's spirit faded completely, the departing soul spoke in a clear voice, "My Emdlen, I may never see your beautiful Atlantis. But promise me this: What you did to prepare me for heaven, where I can at last hear the music of earth and spirit, do this for your people. Do this for as many as you can. For this is the sound you are making, my sweet Emdlen. It is the heart of God that beats in the sound of your voice. Let it beat for them as it has beaten for me."

Emdlen promised. The darkness engulfed him.

When the ship reached the port of Atlantis, Emdlen's father had already been called in advance by the sea patrol and a spectacular reception was waiting. The festivities went on for three days and nights, despite Emdlen's private grief. His crew had consoled him on the last leg of the voyage, but now they all made for their homes and families. On the fourth day, Emdlen went to speak to the Templemaster. He was further dismayed to find that old Ehrgair had died, but Ehrgair had left instructions for his successor, Monjeris.

"So you are Emdlen!" the silver-haired man said, bowing. "I remember you from your days in the choir school." Emdlen prepared to make his request but Monjeris was ready with the questions. "What is the sound the earth is making? What is the sound God is making? And what is the sound you are making?" Monjeris smiled secretively.

"It's a long story," said Emdlen drawing a deep breath. The two of them sat down on cushions facing each other. Monjeris closed his eyes as Emdlen began his tale. By the time Emdlen answered the second question, Monjeris was lifted up, body and soul, into that higher vibrational world where every sound contributes to harmony. There, the sound that every being makes is an explicitly and uniquely perfect version of the sound that God is making. Even after Emdlen had finished speaking, Monjeris did not return to the ordinary plane of this world for hours.

After grieving the death of his beloved well into the following year, Emdlen took the supreme cantor's stand in the Temple for the celebration of the Creation of the Earth ritual. Every inch of congregational space was taken, every ear in Atlantis was attuned to the music of the new cantor. When Emdlen sang that night, every man, woman and child, every living creature, and the entire island of Atlantis itself were lifted up out of the ocean and vanished shimmering into a higher world. Finding his lover there, Emdlen kept singing, and all of Atlantis and its people kept ascending and swirling with them. Evidently, Emdlen is singing still.

Resources

Anonymous, *Meditations on the Tarot* (New York: Element Books, 1989).

Hafiz, *The Subject Tonight Is Love: 60 Wild & Sweet Poems*, Daniel Ladinsky (Myrtle Beach, South Carolina: Pumpkin House Press, 1996).

William Johnston, *Mystical Theology: The Science of Love* (Great Britain: Harper Collins, 1995).

Thomas Merton, *Mystics and Zen Masters* (New York: Delta Book, Dell Pub., 1961).

Runi, *Unseen Rain*, trans. John Moyne and Coleman Barks (Putney, Vermont: Threshold Books, 1986).

Rabindranath Tagore, *Vitanjali: A Collection of Indian Songs*, with an Introduction by W. B. Yeats (New York: Collier Books, 1971).

Thomas Way, *The Way of Chuang Tzu* (New York: New Directions: 1969).

Herbert Weiner, *9½ Mysteries: The Kabbala Today* (New York: Collier Books, 1969).

9

Storytelling in Practice and Performance

———— ✳ ————

This book has looked at the traditions of storytelling—both oral and written—in religion. The process of storytelling involves hearing a story told and making it your own, telling it yourself and then passing it on according to age-old accepted rules and disciplines. The story is passed on from one mouth to another, being transferred to paper only in a shorthand form for memory's sake, or to make the story more singular or detailed in a different form: that of writing.

A story can be taken off a page and put in one's mouth and then into the air, but it is not so easy to do and the inner core can be more easily lost in the process. The difference between reading a story on a page and hearing a story with one's ears is like the difference between reading a script for a play and then seeing that play performed, interpreted and presented. When one hears a story from another, the inner core of the story is honored more truthfully; this is because, in writing, the author's or writer's style has a tendency to usurp the communal tradition. The style of any teller, of course, is always a factor too, but each storyteller bears responsibility for the traditions of storytelling.

The only time a more accurate sense of the meaning of the story can be conveyed in writing is when there is a scribe involved—someone who carefully listens and transcribes what is actually said, almost word for word. In many oral traditions and cultures this is still the case. Storytellers, *griots* (in the African traditions), *senesches* (in the Irish tradition) and many others learn the stories by heart. It is an art that enables one to store an enormous amount of information—plots, characters and events—in one's memory through a process different from rote memorization. That art can be translated into writing by the scribe. Scribes have a special vocation; they disappear into the very words themselves, like the scribes of the early medieval period who copied books line by line, adding their style in the writing, the script, the borders and the embellishments of the letters. The *Lindisfarne Gospels*, the *Book of Kells* and the *Medieval Book of the Hours* are examples of this service and art form. In our own day we have tape recorders and video recorders that allow for word-for-word transcription of the content of the materials and stories. (However, anyone who has listened to tape recordings of stories and then heard the same stories live can sense the startling difference between the live person and the energy that is generated in the listeners and the more "canned" production.)

There is a world of difference between reading and hearing a story. However, the community element that is vital in the oral tradition is very hard, almost impossible to get with your own set of headphones, or watching a video screen. They are, at root, different art forms and different forms of communication.

In this chapter we will look at a number of stories and examine the process of telling a story live, as well as making a written version of it. The first story will be one that began in ears and mouth and then was taped and then finally was transcribed, written down in a form that others could read and appropriate. We will also look at a traditional story from an ancient tradition, a story that was recorded in written form and then taken off the page and put in one person's mouth. Then we will look at a story that was written first for the page, the eye, and then told by the writer orally. We will examine the unique challenges this poses for someone who wishes to tell another's story—one that belongs to a person, rather than to a tradition or a community. The rules are a bit different, but they overlap in many areas.

Finally, we will look at the techniques of telling: voice, content, style, manner, performance. We will examine the disciplines that one must incorporate into one's own lifestyle if one is to be a storyteller within a religious tradition that honors the community that has nurtured the stories and passed them on with a view to extending the life and values of their own beliefs and understandings of the world. We will see how to discover the soul of the story, its spirit, and the style that the story itself demands of any teller. We will learn how to identify the tell-tale signs of betrayal of the story, its tradition, or its maker.

This is basically a "method" chapter, with practical information and rules for being a storyteller, one who collects, tells, and transmits with integrity and honesty. In all religious traditions it is the tale that tells the story and the teller is servant both of the story and the community that inspired the story. To ignore or to break some of the basic rules invalidates the teller and destroys the story and so robs the community of its most valuable resource: its language and its name and claim on the universe. This is arrogance of the highest and most blatant sort. Communities will, though rarely, scorn, exile and exclude someone who does it consistently either for financial gain, reputation or power. Communities will censor that individual teller publicly, declaring that the teller is untrue and does not belong to them or honor their traditions and heart-lines.

This vocation of teller is one of high honor, fraught with responsibility and grace. In general, the oral tradition is stronger and truer, deeper and more meaningful than any written tradition because of its origins in community. The written traditions, such as scriptures, sutras, vedas, and so on are inspired. The depth of the meanings veiled and hidden in the text and its spaces demands that the reader, the hearer, and then eventually the teller dig down deep to discover and reveal the heart of the message and serve it religiously and devotedly. Neither the oral nor the written version of story belongs to any individual. It is borrowed, treasured, and carefully handed on as any other honored ritual or object of devotion. This group of storytellers believes that there is only One

Story, that all stories serve that one story, and that all tellers serve the universal word that invites us and demands that we become truly human and divine.

There is another group of tellers who are purely entertainers or performers. They believe that you can own a story, or take the story out of the mouth of a culture and use it for your own ends, for financial gain, and keep others from telling it, without being responsible to a tradition or a community. Many of these people believe you can own words, even words outside your own culture and language, simply because you tape-recorded them and then wrote them down and published them, without ever acknowledging sources or sharing the financial rewards with those who originally told the stories.

Within both groups of storytellers there is disagreement over whether or not you can own the words of a story, especially as they appear on paper. Legally, the oral version—on tape, on video or in someone's mouth—has priority over the written version (you must tell a story without notes to fall into this category). For this reason, versions of stories in this book and others are either taken from taped versions or told and written by heart onto the page. The original versions of the stories in this book by Tony Cowan and myself are copyrighted in the text as written materials; permission is given to tell them orally in any group with the understanding that you respect the conventions of being a storyteller and honor the religious traditions of any story and its roots in a community.

What follows here is a short compendium of what is called "Teller's Techniques," specifically in regard to storytelling etiquette. It originally appeared in *The Story Bag* newsletter with the rider: "Please feel free to copy this etiquette statement and pass it out or read it at storytelling events."

> Stories are to share and tell. While we encourage the art of sharing stories, we want to encourage respect in our community. You deserve respect. Respect other tellers.
>
> A storyteller's personal, family, and original stories are her/his copyrighted property. It is unethical

and illegal to tell another person's original, personal, and family stories without the permission of the author/storyteller.

Folklore and folktales are owned by the public, but a specific version told by an individual teller or found in a collection is the author's or teller's copyrighted property. If you like a folktale a storyteller has told, ask that teller for a reference or where it can be found. Research the story by finding other versions, and then tell it your way.

Published literary tales and poetry are copyrighted material. They may be told at an informal story swap, but when you tell another's story in a paid professional setting, you need to request the publisher's/author's permission. You need to research copyright law.

When telling anywhere, it is common courtesy to credit the source of your story.

Pass stories, share stories, and encourage respect within the storytelling community.

As Roger Rose, a storyteller from St. Louis, Missouri says: "Respect copyright, but don't be afraid of it."

First a word on listening: the art of listening is hard work, a learned expertise that takes practice. Because of laziness and overly individualized cultural backgrounds, we have a tendency to hear only what we want to hear and we often think we have a right to change specifics to suit our own interests. If you are going to storytell you must train yourself to listen and to hear and to repeat back as much as possible of what was said word for word. Even more important, you must learn to hear with heart, so that you can "heart-speak" out of the depths of your own being and belief and community. N. Scott Momaday, a great Kiowa storyteller and Native American writer, says it thus:

The keepers of the oral tradition had a deeper belief in language than most of us have in general. Language was the repository of their well-being, their

past and their posterity, the irresistible current of their
daily lives. In it their very being was defined and confirmed. And it lay on the plane of the human voice. It
was but one generation from extinction. Words were
necessarily spoken carefully, they were listened to
carefully, and they were remembered carefully. The
alternative was irretrievable loss. (Momaday, pp. 23-
24)

You learn by listening. One of the techniques I have used
over the years to integrate listening almost instinctively in my
work and telling is to repeat what others say—their comments and questions, even if they are long and drawn-out—so
that others can hear it again in my mouth. On tape this is especially important, because usually the quality of the recording is such that if there is no repetition of the comments of the
listeners and participants there is a blank space in the listening, after which the speaker picks up and continues, leaving a
hole in what has been heard. It is not as easy as it might appear and takes years of practice so that it becomes a discipline, but it helps in hearing and retaining stories as well as in
adhering to the heart and the truth of what is spoken.

Now a story! It is a story that is one of my firsts, one that I
have become known for and am often asked to tell over and
over again, even to the same audience. It is unique and singular to my experience, yet it is universal in that all those who
hear it end up seeing and hearing themselves in the event that
I narrate. Long ago I too heard something like it on the west
coast, long before it happened to me. Others often call it "The
Cookie Story," though I refer to it as "Mrs. Fields Chocolate
Chip Cookies." I will put it down on paper as I tell it.

✳   I travel a lot and I have learned some things about airline
travel. First, airlines are forever losing my luggage so I try
to carry essentials with me and if possible take only what
I need. However, when you're on the road for any length
of time, either your suitcase shrinks or your dirty clothes
expand and I seem to be constantly rearranging my suitcase and attaché case in airports, especially after going

through the detectors. Another thing I've learned about traveling is that there are certain airports designed by men (I know it's men); if you go through them, the experience is such that you get rid of all your temporal punishment due to sin. Some of these airports: Chicago, New York's JFK, London, Paris, Rome, Dallas-Fort Worth and Atlanta, especially Atlanta. I used to go through the Atlanta airport so often I thought I lived there and it was always under construction. I was greeted by signs: "Please excuse our mess. We are working to make your experience here a more pleasant one," and so on. Not only that, I would arrive at the airport behind schedule and have to leave from the far end of the terminal (there are four pods). They also have a train that talks to you in an artificial voice: [imitate tram-recorded voice] "This train is about to leave the station. The doors are closing. This train will not leave the station until you move away from the doors." Atlanta is the hub for all military personnel in the United States coming and going, so at any time of the year you will be in the company of people who are miserable and lonely, homesick and nervous, even anxious and afraid of what they are going to or leaving behind.

Well, one day I arrived in the Atlanta airport, tired and grumpy from being on the road for a couple of months, and I was just anxious to get home. The airport was under construction as usual and very crowded. But I smiled and secretly rejoiced because there is one thing that redeems the Atlanta airport: Mrs. Fields chocolate chip cookies!

Now for those of you who do not know about Mrs. Fields cookies there are some things that are essential: first, they are sold not by the cookie, but by weight. They are [use hands to make a fairly large circle] and they come in chocolate chip, mint chocolate chip, white chocolate chip, peanut butter chocolate chip, pecan chocolate chip, and so on. So a dozen of Mrs. Fields' cookies can run you about ten or twelve dollars depending on the weight. But in the south they have this tradition called *lagniappe*, which means something extra, like an extra spoonful of coffee for the pot, or an extra cookie if you buy twelve! So I decided this trip that I deserved a bag, a dozen of Mrs. Fields cookies. So I purchased them and set out to find a place to wait until my flight was called.

Like I said, it was crowded. I went to the waiting area and there was only one chair left in the place: an orange plastic chair with a low plastic table on one side. On the other side of the table there was a black woman sitting. Not just any black woman, mind you, but the biggest black woman I've ever seen. She must have weighed about 300 pounds. She was sitting on the chair, rocking back and forth, with her arms folded and muttering to herself. Next to her on the next three chairs were three skinny little black kids squirming around. Our eyes met (mine and the big woman's) and I went and sat down on the only empty chair.

I put down my bag of Mrs. Fields cookies on the table and bent over and opened my attaché case to re-organize stuff and look through what I needed next. Without thinking, I reached into the bag and took out a cookie and bit into it. It was delicious and I savored it. I was still rooting around in my suitcase and attaché case and out of the corner of my eye I saw this black arm and hand come across the table, reach into my cookie bag, and take one of my cookies! I looked at her and thought: "Hmm, maybe she's hungry," but then thought immediately to myself: "No way, Jose." Still, I figured I could give her one; after all, I had thirteen. But just so she knew whose cookies they were, I looked at her and took another and started chewing. Well, she looked back at me and took three!—one for each of the skinny kids. I thought to myself, "Now they could be hungry," and let it go, but again, to push the point home that these were mine, I took another.

In rapid succession, she took another. I took another. She took three more! I couldn't believe it. In a matter of a few minutes we had managed to snarf down about two pounds of Mrs. Fields cookies. And not only that, she'd had eight of mine and I'd only had four!

Now, besides this, there were all kinds of "conversations" going on between me and the other people sitting in the waiting room. They were rolling their eyes and shaking their heads, laughing and trying to keep from laughing, making faces—and I was responding back, and trying to keep some sort of composure. And I was thinking, "I only have one more cookie. She wouldn't dare!"

And then...I don't believe it! Out comes that black arm and into my bag goes her hand. She takes out my last Mrs. Fields cookie, looks me right in the eye, breaks my last cookie in half, and gives me half!

I took it and ate it just as they called my flight. I got up, threw my empty bag of Mrs. Fields into the trash can, picked up my bag and attaché case and headed down the runway. The last thing I saw when I looked back was her sitting there on that chair, arms folded, rocking back and forth and muttering to herself, and the three skinny kids waving to me. And I got on the plane.

Now one of the problems of being a theologian is that you think that everything that happens to you has significant meaning and I was thinking: something important just happened to me, but I haven't a clue what it is! The Old Testament tells us that God comes to visit in the guise of a stranger and if this was God, how did I do? Well, I did give her eight and a half of my cookies, though I wasn't all that gracious about it, the way I was thinking. Or maybe she was just strange! I couldn't figure out exactly what had gone on. But I journal a lot and write letters on planes and sometimes when I write I can figure out what is going on. We sat on the runway for ages and finally we took off. Eventually I put my tray table down and reached down to open my attaché case to get pencil and paper and write about it. I found pencil and paper all right— AND MY BAG OF MRS. FIELDS CHOCOLATE CHIP COOKIES! I couldn't believe it! I put the bag of cookies on the tray and just looked at them and thought: O my God! that woman must think I'm crazy. I ate her cookies! [Pause, usually off and on, during the last few sentences for howling laughter] No wonder she was muttering to herself when I left. She was probably thinking, "Strange white women, never can tell what they're up to." Then I thought, "How stupid could I be!" And I knew with my luck that if I ever came through Atlanta again, I'd meet her! Or worse, on the way into the kingdom she'd be standing there pointing at me as I approached the gates! I was so damm self-righteous, there was no way I could ever let someone find out what I had done. So, I promptly bribed God (one resorts to infantile behavior at these moments of insight and incredulity) and I promised God that if no one ever found out what I'd done, I'd never eat a Mrs. Fields cookie ever again.

The cookies sat on the tray all the way to San Francisco. When I got off, I went down the runway and as I walked past people waiting to meet others on the plane I handed out cookies: "Would you like a cookie? Would you like a cookie?"

Well, about a week later, I was in Ghiradelli Square and wouldn't you know it—there's a Mrs. Fields cookie store. I walked past it a number of times, resisting. But at heart I'm a weak person and I began to try to figure a way to renege on my bribe-promise. Finally, I succumbed and went in, and as I bit into that delicious cookie, I promised myself that every time I ate a Mrs. Fields cookie I would tell the story of the woman in the Atlanta airport, ending with the line, "Whenever you are dead sure you're right about something, watch it! You could be dead wrong and you could be eating somebody else's cookies!"

That's the story—and it's very hard to write down, though I pretty much tell it exactly the same way every time. It's a pattern, a rhythm, and it was learned along with learning when to stop for the laughter to subside. I've given all sorts of people permission to tell this story and they can't! They try, but they just can't, because they put it in the third person and it loses its sock. So, I've told them to tell it in the first person (the hardest kind of story to tell generally) and then it works. I suggest that they tell the story as closely as possible to the way I do, beginning with the first rule of storytelling,

"All stories are true; some of them actually happened," and launching into it. After they tell the story and the laughter dies away, then they can tell the group that it didn't really happen to them, but to me. They can remind hearers of the fact that they are not necessarily laughing at me when they hear it, but at themselves for being caught out, for connecting with and remembering similar circumstances in their own lives, incidents that they found equally appalling. Timing is of utmost importance in this story, knowing when to slow down and when to draw it out. Above all, it's important to do it deadpan as if you're not doing anything weird—*she* is! It takes practice.

Easier stories to tell are found in the religious traditions, precisely because they are not so personal and intimately connected to you as the teller and you are not as heavily invested in either the telling or the outcome. All religious stories (and that includes many more than one would initially think) have certain shared characteristics. Once when I was in St. Louis to tell stories to hundreds of school children (a different group every fifty minutes) at an annual festival, I attended a cocktail party the night before to meet other storytellers in an informal setting. We had received our programs and were going over who was doing what kind of storytelling. I introduced myself to someone, a teller with a New York radio program, and when he heard my name he responded: "Oh, you're the one who does religious stories." It was said with obvious disdain and an air of infinite superiority. I was a bit put out but didn't reply right away; in fact, I was biting my tongue. Then, from behind me came a deep strong voice that spoke with authority, saying: "Oh, I didn't know there was any other kind." I turned to find a bear of a man—literally wearing a necklace of bear claws—towering over me with a wide open face and smile. He introduced himself as Joe Bruchac, an Abenaki-Polish storyteller from upstate New York, and ever since I have admired his quick response and wisdom. These stories often have all of the following characteristics.

First there is a mixture of *chronos* time and *kairos* time: ordinary time and time out-of-time that draws you into forever. Second, there is an element of judgment in the story, revealing values, ethics or morals from a tradition. This judgment is about rebalancing, repairing and standing in the breach in a world that struggles with good and evil. Third, the presence of a community looms in the text, or in the context, the background of those whose story it is and/or of the listeners. Community announces that together we are most like God, specifically in the Christian tradition that Trinity, who God is, is what we are also challenged to become here on earth. Fourth, paradoxes abound, especially that of justice and mercy overlaid together, insinuating that everything in the world is redeemable, though often at great price. Fifth, the truth must be told, words must be set free, certain groups must be defended and given a voice. This is tied very closely to remembrance that there are always spirit-filled alternatives to the dominant realities. The alternatives are prophetic, mystical and freeing and the very telling purges a small place of evil and injustice or insensitivity. Sixth, the story has a universal quality to it, crossing all sorts of boundaries of time, place, culture, race, language, religious belief, gender lines, and so on. It is about making community, about drawing in outsiders, strangers and those exiled or slipping off as fringe. Seventh is the dynamic of the transcendent and the immanence of the holy, the divine and the transforming. This is the strong mixture of body and soul, matter and spirit, incarnation both in the content of the story and in the bodies of the teller and the listeners. Eighth is the demand that the stories must make for peace, for joy and for a world without violence. Often the stories incorporate either a ferocious nonviolent resistance to evil or a hope embodied in people who are willing to sacrifice everything, though they obviously love life, so that others may have a chance to live too.

I often tell people that we are known by the stories we tell and the company we keep, keeping in mind that the word company denotes those with whom we journey and those with whom we break bread—what we choose to do with our money and resources. These are the core elements that proclaim who we are, what we cherish and value, what we seek to make real in our own lives and pass on.

Some practical considerations, short and to the point. First, in preparing to tell a story:

1. Know the setting and something of the main characteristics. Study its ideas.
2. Outline the story (big action—climax—resolution—conclusion). In addition to the words, phrases, paraphrases, and repetitions, study the context (the before and after elements that often hold the clue to the point of a passage).
3. Read the story and know its vantage point. Understand it and take it to heart. Know the sequence of events. Then learn the story by heart, not memorizing it.
4. Rehearse the story inside you at odd moments during the day, at night, walking, until you can't get enough of it.
5. Rehearse it out loud and time it. Stay faithful to the story.
6. Use natural spontaneous gestures. Try them out first alone and then look at yourself in a mirror, or ask someone to watch you.
7. Use your eyes.
8. Work with silences, pauses, transitions, contrasts.
9. Practice breathing to be fluid and loose.
10. Use tone, pitch, volume, rate, emphases, whispers, sighs, sounds. Gain momentum.
11. Be sincere.
12. Tell it each time as though it were the first time. Listen to it yourself. The hardest moment is the beginning. Breathe, gather yourself (you learn your own ritual) and begin: "Once upon a time..."
13. Keep stories on cards; collect them. I have sheets that list one phrase or line or even just one word that triggers the entire story for me.
14. Rotate, but do tell stories again and again. They have layers of insight and power like a seven-layer cake, at least.
15. Allow for mistakes and failure. Laugh at yourself and remember that everything is redeemable!
16. Listen to others' stories, the ones they tell publicly, the ones they cherish and give away to carefully chosen

folk only on special occasions. Listen to the stories of birds, events, earth and sky.

17. Remember—this is not just an art, but a discipline and a way of life. Practice makes for knowledge, ease and grace. With time and diligence, the story comes true in you first, inviting all who listen to come true too.

In regard to scripture and storytelling, the things to know and practice also include these:

1. Know what the author wants to communicate and wonder how you can do it most tellingly and truthfully, so the experience is shared.

2. It has to move you, touch you personally, convince and convert you or be about something that you passionately believe in and want to express more fully.

3. Learn the materials of the craft: both basic exegesis, moving, timing, pacing, using your own voice and what is born of the spirit. What makes a story is mysterious.

4. Excavate a story. Dig your way back to the original and what sparked the writer.

5. Be disciplined. Stick with the structure of the story and make scripture a daily part of your life personally as well as publicly or in performance.

6. Don't take yourself seriously. Take the scripture and people—both the people in the story and your listeners—very seriously.

7. A story throws people and events together in a moment of awareness, crisis, insight, interchange, conversion or transformation. It it's good it probes, it exposes human nature. Watch for these qualities: immanence, hope, and judgment.

8. Be creative and remember why you're telling the story—so others can hear and be caught up in the wonder and wisdom of the Word of God.

9. Work at it, find your way, think of it as a maze, a pilgrimage, a journey into meaning.

10. Let the story tell you! And keep in mind the understanding of what all stories do: they turn hearts and

turn history inside out and over. The teller is a midwife to the tradition in the lives of listeners.

To tell stories and act them out, or to make them come true for others to hear and see, you have to keep in mind some crucial realities.

1. Realize that *you* are capable of great evil.
2. The dark is rising; you must stand with the light. And yet, paradoxically, the night is also holy, allowing you to see the stars and appreciate the light.
3. You can tell the story of the struggle only with art: with dance, mime, song, laughter, sighs, instruments, and other art forms.
4. Let go and touch genuine joy and gladness, giving others permission to experience all the ranges of emotion also.
5. Be in contact with contraries: joy/despair, a kind of madness and holiness.
6. Go through your own journey and tell out of that experience, but not that experience: universalize it. Francis met a leper. Whom have you met? Dig to find the stranger in you.
7. You have to go back and tell people of the great things that God has done for you, for your story is for others and, once they have it, they can do what is necessary for them. It is no longer just yours. Be generous and don't put too much of you in it.
8. Change comes with mystic imagination and experience. Death and resurrection are what we're always talking about and revealing as the inner structure of all of reality.
9. Press the text and spin the details, staying close to the truth.
10. Love it madly!

With stories, time stops; space stretches; reality is intensified; what is told happens again; community is re-membered; all are reconciled and judged; people are empowered and told the truth. Stories belong to all. In fact, it is said and believed by many that this is really why God became human: he loved our stories and wanted more and more to be a part of them and us coming true.

Now another story. This one was written for the page first and then lifted off the page and put into the writer's mouth. Note the differences in finding a story on a page and listening to it told again (the tape version). It is called "The Dragon-Prince: A Fairy Tale" and it was written and told by Tony Cowan.

✳   Once upon a time, there was a land in which the people were terrified of a roaming dragon. They complained bitterly to the king, saying it was his duty to rid the kingdom of this menace. The king agreed. He had his eldest son fitted with titanium armor and dispatched him to slay the beast. But the next day, the prince's body was found lying lifeless under a tree. So the king sent out his second son, armed with a titantium suit plus a flamethrower, to kill the dragon. But the next day, the prince's body was found at the bottom of a cliff. Finally, the king sent his youngest son, armed with a titanium suit, a flamethrower and a flashlight, to destroy the monster. The next day his body was found floating down a river. The king had no more sons. While he was walking in his orchard, despondently wondering what to do and nibbling a tart Golden Delicious, the king's daughter appeared.

Now, the king's daughter had always been a strange, strong-willed spirit who loved to climb trees, explore caves, and fix diesel engines. She approached the king and announced, "I want to go meet the dragon." The king's jaws locked and his cheeks bulged with apple flesh. He looked stern and unyielding.

"You are going nowhere, young lady," he retorted, swallowing hard. "That dragon has killed your brothers. What chance would *you* have?" But, as the king expected, his daughter became adamant and would not drop the subject. So the king, knowing how strong-willed she was, locked her up in the castle tower "for her own protection."

That night, the princess lowered herself from the tower window, using her long, retractable Rapunzel hair. As she stole away into the forest to seek the dragon, the lamp of her desire outshone the little wrought-iron lantern she toted. And so, she looked and wandered, looked and wandered, until in the deepest, stillest thicket of the woods, she heard a hissing and a sighing like an unlit oxy-acetylene torch. It was coming from the depths of an enormous cave. The princess tip-toed to the mouth of the cave and started in and down, in and down, her eyes adjusting with the failing glow of the lantern. The breathing grew steadily louder. Then the princess froze. Before her lay the gigantic mass of a sleeping dragon, his body a mound of blacker shadow. Just at that moment, her lamp went out. The princess had not expected to make contact with the dragon this way. Fearing to rouse him, and overcome by the warmth of the cave and the hypnotic breathing of the beast, the princess lay down next to the wall and fell asleep. Unknown to either the princess or the dragon, during the night they moved, turned, and stretched in their sleep so that by dawn they were nestled tightly together. In fact, they were sharing the same breaths (which can be terribly dangerous with dragons).

As the dusty rays of dawn shot into the belly of the cave and onto their slumbering bodies, the princess and the dragon awoke, nose-to-nose, at exactly the same moment. Startled by the presence of a human being, the dragon sucked in a quick breath but held its fire. Startled by the presence of the dragon, the princess also drew in a sharp breath. At that moment, there was just enough light for the princess to see that, close up, the dragon was not hideously ugly, but had skin like oiled leather, glittering red and green and black, as if there were tiny rubies, jades and onyxes embedded there. Exhilarated, the princess leaned forward until her nose touched the dragon's, and she gave it a passionate kiss, as if it were her very last.

Suddenly, a roaring wind filled the cave. Flashes and sparks rained down and smoke billowed in blinding profusion. Terrified, the princess crouched down, pressing her face and hands into the ground as it quaked beneath her. She was beside herself with fright. Someone's life flashed before her eyes. She waited and waited, expecting to be crushed, diced or flambéed. But presently, everything became quiet in the cave, and the dust and smoke settled. The princess lifted her face from the ground and gave a dry, little cough. Bathed in the soft, amber sunlight, there, where the dragon had been, lay the naked body of a young man more handsome than the gods and bearing a prince's crown. Before he regained consciousness, she covered him with her long retractable Rapunzel hair and several more passionate kisses, as if they were her very first.

The princess and the dragon-prince spent many days and nights walking through the forest, falling in love. One day, they emerged and walked back to the castle and into the throne room.

The king was not there. They found him in the cemetery grieving for his children. After he had made a great fuss over his daughter, she exclaimed, "Father, not only has the dragon disappeared from your kingdom, but I have found a prince to succeed you. Indeed, I have broken a powerful spell. Behold the prince who was once a dragon!"

The king was astonished. The prince explained, "In my father's kingdom, I refused to fight, to practice war, and to go out and slay our dragons. Eventually, my father grew so enraged that he put a curse on me and sent me into exile. As I crossed the castle drawbridge, I turned into a dragon. But, even as a dragon, I refused to kill people. I am sorry about your sons. They were murdered by titanium thieves."

The king frowned. When he asked his daughter the princess how she had survived her encounter with the dragon, she said firmly, "Everything terrible is, in its deepest being, something that wants our help."

Now, the king did not entirely understand but, even so, until his final days he was bathed in the radiance of this gentle truth. And they say that once upon a time, there was a land where dragons were no longer terrified of people. The End. (This story was inspired by Rainer Maria Rilke).

When a tale starts on paper it has a different flavor, a more pronounced style. Since it reaches for the eye first, it is tighter. It reveals the writer's culture, education, nationality and, in this instance, sense of humor and playfulness. So to tell the story is to imitate the overall sense and feel of the story from another's point of view. It is like acting, borrowing another's way of perceiving and living in the world. Generally speaking, stories of your own experience or stories of other people who are contemporaries are the most difficult to tell, either because of emotional involvement or the peculiarity of the creator or the requirement of having to learn another's style before sharing that person's story with others. In between are the stories usually referred to as folktales. These can be found in various countries, and are marked by touches of local color. They travel across oceans and centuries with ease, because they have a common human thread that preserves the meaning while changing the characters and setting to conform with an environment. Just reading or hearing such a story will call forth a familiar ring or echo suggesting that you've heard something like that before, in this case the echoes of the German poet Rainer Maria Rilke's lines about dragons.

This story is a mix of a particular writer and the genre of fairytale in a more contemporary fantasy mode. The writer's British education can probably be detected, as well as other distinguishing qualities (tongue-in-cheek wit, and a strange twist to an old tale).

The group of stories that is most common is made up of those that originate in the oral voice of a people, a religion and a community: those found in the great religious traditions of the world. These stories seem to carry universal beliefs and hopes and tell of the long and ancient wisdom gleaned from those before us and their struggles and dreams. These stories belong to a people and so, once their heritage and lineage are acknowledged, they can be told to almost everyone.

When choosing a story to tell, the first rule is that you must love the story, have been enchanted by its telling and meaning, are intrigued by its layers, and want to learn how to let the story seep into you so that it can tell you and pass on its truth and wisdom. You will find that as you grow you will tell stories again and again, or lose them and let them go their way. A story you once passed over will be one that later touches a place uncovered by an experience in your life, or that will move you because of its impassioned telling by someone else. And there are some stories you will never be able to tell: because you don't understand them, or because they offend you, or because they do not speak to you. Other reasons for not telling a story: length, local dialect, lack of awareness of a world or religious view that undergirds the story, recognition of the danger or threat posed by a story at a given point in your life. Trust your intuitions and beware telling a story just because you need to have a story or something new. Make sure of the heart-lines and have a good grasp of the story or the telling can be disastrous and unpleasant.

Bottom line: be true to the story and to yourself, in equal measures. There is a knowledge learned the hard way by storytellers, and it is this: you become the stories you tell. It is very hard to separate the teller from the tale in the minds of those who listen and either take them to heart or reject them. The story comes true when you do too.

Resources

Brian Cavanaugh, TOR, *The Sower's Seeds* (Mahwah, NJ: Paulist Press, 1990). Note this is a series of four books.

Barbara Griffin, Olga Loya, Sandra MasLees, Nancy Schimmel, Harlynne Geisler and Kathleen Zundell, "Teller's Techniques," in *The Story Bag* newsletter, July 1993 (5361 Javier St., San Diego CA 92117-3215).

Ruthilde Kronberg and Patricia McKissack, *A Piece of the Wind And Other Stories to Tell* (New York: Harper and Row, 1990).

Margaret Read MacDonald, *The Story-tellers Start-Up Book: Finding, Learning, Performing and Using Folktales* (Little Rock, AR: August House, 1993).

Jack Maguire, *Creative Storytelling: Choosing, Inventing and Sharing Tales for Children* (New York: McGraw Hill, 1985).

Joseph F. Martin, *Foolish Wisdom, Stories, Activities, and Reflections from Ken Feit* (San Jose, CA: Resource Publications, 1990).

Nancy Mellon, *Storytelling and the Art of Imagination* (Rockport, MA: Element, 1992).

N. Scott Momaday, as quoted by Gerald Hausman, "'Listening,' The Tribal Art of Storytelling," *Forkroads* (Winter, 1995).

Ruth Sawyer, *The Way of the Storyteller* (New York: Viking Press, 1942).

Joseph Sherman, *Once Upon a Galaxy: Ancient Stories behind Star Wars, Superman and Other Popular Fantasies* (Little Rock, AR: August House, 1994).

Ruth Stotter, *About Story: Writings on Stories and Storytelling, 1980-1994* (Stinson Beach, CA: Stotter Press, 1994). Also an annual "Storyteller's Calendar" is available from Stotter Press (P.O. Box 726, Stinson Beach CA 94970 @ $10.00, +$2.00 S&H).

Theophane the Monk, *Tales of the Magic Monastery* (New York: Crossroads, 1981).

William R. White, *Stories for Telling: A Treasury of Christian Storytellers* (Minneapolis: Augsburg, 1986).

10

Opening Your Mouth and Coming True

———— ✳ ————

Of all that God has shown me I can speak just the
     smallest word,
Not more than a honey bee
Takes on his food
From an overspilling jar.
     (Mechtild of Magdeburg)

After you had taken your leave, I found God's
footprints on my floor. (Tagore)

We can make our minds so like still water that be-
ings gather about us, that they may see their own
images, and so live for a moment with a cleaner,
perhaps even with a fiercer, life because of our
quiet. (William Butler Yeats)

Storytelling is an art. It is a basic to communication. Some
say it is essential to our survival as human beings. Buckminster
Fuller used to tell this simple story as a prelude to many of his
talks to scientists and anthropologists. Once upon a time a man
wanted to know what was the essence of humanity, the essential core ingredient of a human being. He worked in a high-tech
computer lab, servicing the equipment, and at times the big
computer was taken off line. At one such time he thought to

ask it the question: What is core to being human? He typed in the question and the computer went to work. Well, it worked for hours, night and day, assessing all the available information. The man was worried. The computer, being multi-faceted, did other jobs, but all its spare time was spent funneling back into his question. For weeks the computer worked on it and finally it downloaded the answer, spitting it out. It read: "Once upon a time . . ." It is clever, but to the point.

Stories are crucial to our sense of well-being, to identity, to memory, and to our future. There is a power to stories that can often be experienced as one listens—sometimes even more so when one is telling them—but it is hard to put into words just what that power is and how it operates. There is a skill to storytelling. Underneath that skill is the inherent magic and wisdom of the story itself and of its crafting over generations of telling and being heard. This power is not to be underestimated, especially by those of us in the age of electronic information, computers and technical expertise, or else we will lose something irreplaceable.

Marie Louise van Franz, in her introduction to *The Interpretation of Fairy Tales* tells of a custom among the Australian aborigines: "When the rice does not grow well the women go into the ricefield and squat among the rice and tell it the myth of the origin of the rice. Then the rice knows again why it is there and grows like anything." Some may think this quaint, and scoff, but there are others who still believe that the world is made of stories and that the telling is, literally, what keeps the world together and all of existence and life from growing faint or extinct. Stories save our lives on basic levels and on levels of great subtlety and depth.

In the old collection of stories called *The Tales from the Thousand and One Nights* we find the story of the woman Scheherazade, one in a long line of women brought to a king who sleeps with them for only one night and then has them executed. But Scheherazade is not only beautiful, she is enchanting. She begins by telling the king a story. The king is bored and depressed. He is without imagination, and so he is cruel and inhuman, but at once he is caught in the magical power of the story. And for a thousand and one nights it is Scheherazade who holds the king captive and gives him back a life worth living, with meaning. She tells him stories that make him laugh and cry, think and reflect. She tells him stories of bravery and cowardice, of truth and falsehood, and of those who have endured, remained faithful and stood against all odds to return to those they love or to defend what they believe in. He is entertained, educated, sensitized and made human. In fact, he falls in love with the storyteller and realizes that he wants her as his queen. She has worked magic on him: ancient, wise, understanding magic. She has made him a peace-maker, just and compassionate, and in the process has saved her life and the lives of many others. In waiting for the tale every evening and remembering it throughout the day he is drawn in, down and further into the mystery of life and love. The story of Scheherazade reminds us that this experience is a reality in all of our lives to one extent or another.

Elie Wiesel, writer and commentator on the human condition, has told stories that almost defy understanding about the Holocaust and our own inhumanity to one another as well as stories of wild hope, belief and sustaining and transforming love in the midst of suffering and evil. He respects the power of words and especially that of storytelling. In his Nobel Prize acceptance speech he said,

> No one is as capable of gratitude as one who has emerged from the kingdom of the night.
>
> We know that every moment is a moment of grace, every hour an offering; not to share them would mean to betray them. Our lives no longer belong to us alone; they belong to all those who need us desperately...
>
> And that is why I swore never to be silent whenever and wherever human beings endure suffering and humiliation. We must always take sides. Neutrality helps the oppressor, never the victim. Silence encourages the tormentor, never the tormented.

This is one of the reasons why we tell stories. And many who tell such stories are considered "trouble-makers," because they are dangerous enough to dream hope for the human race and give voice to those whose tongues are tied and whose hearts are constricted and whose lives are oppressed. The Jewish prophets were persecuted and brought down in Jerusalem. Jesus of Nazareth was crucified in an attempt to silence his words. Countless martyrs in every religion have refused to let others tear their dreams from them even as these others took their breath and life. Sufi poets and mystics, contemporary truth-tellers like Gandhi, Martin Luther King, Oscar Romero and scores of unnamed though not-forgotten people are among those whose words were not silenced but poured into the ground and the air about us. Their last story—and often their best—was their most striking and powerful: the one that chronicled forever their deaths and entrance into that great silence of forever more.

Here are two stories of trouble-makers who know the power of story, of the word spoken and the word worth remembering enough to write down, to capture on a page so that it can be told again and again and live in the imaginations and hearts of others world-wide. The first is from a man who is alive and well. Eduardo Galeano, born in Uruguay in 1940, is an editor, writer, storyteller and one of Latin America's best known social analysts who looks at the world from the vantage point of the southern hemisphere and speaks from his heart. This excerpt is from a speech he gave to the World Congress of Christian Communicators about two years ago. It appeared originally in Spanish in *Pastoral Popular*.

The loaves and fishes have never been more unequally distributed. The system which rules the world, the one so antiseptically referred to as "market economy," is allowed to act with ever greater impunity. Today poverty can generate pity but it no longer provokes indignation. The poor are poor because of the rules of the game and the dice of destiny. Up until 20 or 30 years ago poverty was seen as the fruit of injustice. It was denounced by the left, admitted by the centre, and rarely denied by the right. Now poverty is the punishment for inefficiency or merely an expression of the natural order of things. Poverty has now been separated from injustice and even the very notion of injustice, something universally unaccepted in the recent past, has been so modified that it almost disappears...

The same thing happens with violence as happens with poverty. In the south of our planet where the losers live, violence is rarely presented as the result of injustice. Violence is almost always exhibited as the result of the bad conduct of those third-class types of people who inhabit the so-called Third World. Isn't that part of their nature! Things were always like that and always will be. Violence, like poverty, is attributed to the natural order.

I listened to this man tell stories of Latin America and its long history of struggle, of injustice and hope for dignity; of people ancient and ordinary who have sought only to live with a future for their children, food for the day and a sense of the beauty of the earth. His images stay in the mind. In describing the economic, political, and even racial tension and history of South America he used his hand, with the five fingers spread wide apart. This is the way the railroads were built, with each long finger snaking into a different geographical location: one to take out the ore, another for the oil, another for the corn and crops, another for cattle, another for human slaves. But none of them was connected to the others. This was deliberate. There was no interest in development, interdependence, communication or simple travel for the indigent. The goal was to bleed an entire continent dry, sucking its life out systematically over the decades. It was a hand of death, strong and grasping and white. As I sat and listened I was ashamed. I heard a voice that cried out in anger, that would not let the dominant interpretation of reality prevail.

This is another reason to tell stories: to speak the truth and exhort us to do justice and make peace; to disturb the status quo that accepts inhuman acts and situations and tolerates violence and subhuman living conditions for the majority of the human race. Stories can trouble us, disturb our false sense of security and self-righteousness and jolt us out of our numb and complacent pockets of unreality. When questioned before Pilate about what truth is, Jesus—who was described by the early Christian community as the Way, the Truth and the Life—answered that all who hear his voice know the truth and that this is the very reason why he was born. Jesus is a born storyteller and though those who abhor or are afraid of the truth have their hour, there is also the time of the storyteller and the time for truth.

Another storyteller and preacher, a man beloved of his people, has himself become the subject of stories because he was converted in response to the stories of others, friends and people he ministered to and who ministered to him as well. This man was Oscar Romero, the slain archbishop of San Salvador, who learned to listen to the stories of others and so to have his ears opened and his heart laid bare to the truth. In return he lent these others his voice for a period of time before the military and the mighty stilled that voice, though not the presence and the memory of the man. John Donaghy, a friend of mine who spends a good deal of time in El Salvador collecting the stories of those who survived the period of distress of the 1980s and '90s, has shared this story with me. It is entitled "The Bible: A Book of Subversion."

❊   Elvira Rodriguez told of being in the Legion of Mary. The Legion of Mary, active throughout the world, is a fairly traditional apostolate for the laity. Members go and visit people, encouraging them to participate in the life of the church. In Suchitoto, however, group members would meet to reflect on the Bible. But the Bible was considered a subversive book. So when the police or soldiers were near, people got very quiet. They were afraid of being caught by the soldiers during these biblical reflections.

Elvira told of a relative who was a catechist. One day he was stopped and arrested by the police. He was carrying a communist book: a Bible with red covers.

Others also told of this. In the summer of 1992 I was helping Sister Carol with the training of new catechists in the far western zone of the parish. As we finished the first lesson, Carol asked if they had Bibles. Some of the women said they used to have Bibles, but they had to hide them. One woman recounted the story of the woman who was reading the Bible when soldiers stormed into her house and killed her. This woman swore it was the truth.

There is a story told by Antonio Fernandez Ibanez in *Piezas para un retrato* that bears repeating:

* I was out visiting a canton of Aguilares with four campesinos, one of them the famous Polin [Apolinario Serrano]. "Let's get together for a short time to study the Bible," one of them said.

"And why doesn't the priest come along with us?" asked Polin.

"That sounds good. I'm free this afternoon. Let's go, then," I told them, and we went out walking until we found ourselves under the shade of a rubber tree. We were some distance from the houses. All around we could only see countryside.

"Shall we take it out?"

"Get it."

They had hidden the Bible, buried it in the earth in a sack made of plastic bags. In those days the Bible was one of the most subversive books that one could possess. Frequently the army would kill anyone with a Bible.

People used to come here and meet to read and reflect on St. John's Gospel. They took the Bible out of the plastic and opened it.

"And you," they said, "pay attention. Listen if we say something that's really just nonsense. You know. Set us right."

They read, they commented on the text, they sat there in silence as if praying, they talked. And I was all eyes and ears listening to them. More than an hour had passed when, all of a sudden, in the distance we saw a speck that was moving and getting closer.

"There's nothing to worry about. It's just an animal."

They continued reading, but kept glancing out of the corner of their eyes. "What's going to happen? It's a person." They were alarmed and hid the Bible in a pile of leaves.

"It's a woman. She's wearing a skirt."

"What a skirt! It's a priest's cassock!"

"It *is* a priest!"

And it got closer...

"It's Archbishop Romero!" He was coming closer, walking all alone along those trails. "Archbishop, what are you doing walking around here?"

"And I say, 'What are all of you doing here?' "

"We're reading the Bible, St. John's Gospel."

"And are you going to let your pastor sit down with you?" he asked them.

"Here, all we've got is a big chair," Polin answered.

He sat down in a little grassy area. And they continued for another hour with their reflection—reading calmly, speaking calmly, like campesinos do, all well thought-through so that their talk doesn't end up like idle chatter. Archbishop Romero didn't open his mouth. When they were finished, I turned and saw that his eyes were wet—he was crying.

"What happened, Archbishop?"

"I thought I knew the Gospel, but I'm learning how to read it in a different way." And there was Polin, the rascal, smiling. (Lopez Vigil, pp. 253-54)

To hear old stories from new mouths, and to be open in mind and heart sets loose the spirit of the story afresh in the world, a spirit that may have lain dormant and still, waiting for the kiss of appreciation and love to awaken it once again. In order to be a good storyteller, you must first know how to listen and let the story capture you. And as the heart of a story is discovered, it begins to become incarnated in the teller. In a word, we become the stories we love and tell the most.

The Christian tradition proclaims that The Word became Flesh and dwells among us. In response we, with our words of belief, of assent, of shared hope, must become flesh for others' food. Our flesh must bear witness to the presence of words instilled and cherished, believed and borne witness to in commitment, example and service, and sometimes in the giving of life itself as the final word. It is still the best story, the only story worth telling. It is the one that declares silently and in every language that exists that all is redeemable and life is stronger than death, friendship is truer than hate and non-violent resistance is more powerful than destruction and blind fury. When all is said and done, the truth will be told by those who are storytellers at heart, those who incarnate the words they believe so that all can heed and take note.

There is an ancient Chinese story I heard from a Taoist priest when I was in Japan that tells it deftly.

＊ Once upon a time there was an ancient potter, a national treasure if ever there was one, a master of glaze and form in the making of porcelain vases and pots. He was obsessed with beauty, with finding the perfect color and hue, tone and depth. He was always searching out new grades of sand, or testing the level of fire in his kilns, trying the glazes at each gradation of temperature and noting the subtle differences. But he felt that exquisite beauty—perfection—eluded him no matter how diligently and consistently he worked at his craft and art. He exhausted his funds, his ideas and his imagination in his attempt to capture, if only once, on one set of pots the glaze that would make any who caught a glimpse of it sigh in admiration and wondrous awe. And then he knew what was next, the only thing he could do: he fired up the flames of the kiln to a white hot pitch and walked into the kiln. He disappeared.

The next day his students took out the pieces that had been in the kiln, vases, pots, bowls and large plates. They carried them in awe, because they almost seemed alive. They had the most serene and powerful glazes that anyone had ever seen. Their beauty was beyond description. The master had finally achieved his dream by adding his flesh and spirit to the mix. Finally he had discovered the secret knowledge: one must somehow become what one desires and loves.

It is a universal truth, sought yet drawn back from, approached and avoided at our cores. Meister Eckhart puts it in Christian theological terms: "Jesus became a human being because God, the compassionate one, could not suffer and lacked a back to be beaten. God needed a back like ours on which to receive blows and thereby to perform compassion as well as to preach it. However great one's suffering is, if it comes through God, God suffers from it first." There are many who would say that any suffering, even at the hands of others, is matter for spirit to transform. It can be transformed if the one who bears the suffering seeks to love, and is willing to extend that love even to the one responsible for the suffering. So many of the traditions say that this is the story of God and that all the other stories are practice for this one. All the stories seek to crack our souls, to bend the knees of our heart, to wake us up and teach us how to walk through time with "sufficient carelessness" (a phrase borrowed from Thoreau). And the stories told in the context—or against the backdrop—of fear, pain, oppression, violence and loss are the most powerful stories. They are the ones told when almost everything is already lost and enduring with grace and passing on truth, even if one does not survive, is the only imperative.

These stories put first the needs of the meek and the terrorized. They are filled with a moral sense of human obligation for others less fortunate who might disappear forever if we do not speak. And they are told to honor fidelity, the fidelity that integrates our words, actions and presence into one statement that is about being human and full of grace in the midst of horror and death.

In this tradition and experience each story—whether found in a treasured text or still cocooned in the oral tradition—is a ritual, a healing event that weaves together wisdom and action, the finite and the infinite, the world beyond and all the worlds in between. The breath of the telling keeps the fire alive in the world and sends forth sparks of wisdom. The story, then, is a vessel that codifies and transmits vital information, the innermost secrets of the heart. It speaks from and to a place of hiddenness where God seeks refuge and longs for us to come to know what is divine and holy.

This kind of knowing comes not just from the words and the telling. It also comes from the long discipline and apprenticeship of enfleshing, incarnating the content into flesh and bone and blood so that it can come true again in this time and place. The adage is true: the story begins when the teller stops talking! The story has a momentum and continues on in you, in us, in all who listen, who hear and who take it to heart. It is an eternal momentum that increases in power as it touches more and more people through time.

The transformation of the story is a process that begins with the oral tradition. It is written down, enshrined as Torah, as scripture, as Sutra, and then it becomes at last the living word in a person. This is the story coming true, being transformed into the most excellent text of all. It is a text not only to be read and listened to; it is a text in whose presence one can stand.

Such stories strive for "holy joy," a shiver that goes through your soul. They herald a way of knowing realities worth staking your life on, even dying for, realities that confirm universal truths and—above all—make us remember what it means to be human and made by God's hands and breath.

A story with insight, with meaning, is as inspired as any text in a tradition. Each time, each telling, each listening is new and stirs up emotion and courage to act. The story knows and gives away the deepest knowledge to any who need to hear and can let it find a home within. We listen to stories to remember who we are and to be urged once again to divine service in our human encounters, to holiness, obedience and awe of what is divine, to love, to devotion, to compassionate justice—to all those things that hardly anybody really knows or practices.

The story has hidden wisdom that often can travel only by word of mouth, person to person, prophet to disciple (as in the case of Elijah's transmission to Elisha as a double portion of spirit), master to student, friend to friend, the Friend to beloved. This is the work of the Spirit shared with storytellers: to carefully guard the transmission of telling and translating the truth, imagining it anew in each generation and people so

that the possibilities of life do not wither and die out from mis-
use or get lost in the scuffle of other concerns and interests.
The word is carried on the welcoming wind of breath, sigh,
song, silence and articulation that creates as powerfully as it
did at the moment of creation. The voice is in reality more per-
manent than the written word, for it is the voice that brings the
story to life, using the power of the moment, the presence of
the listeners, and the need that draws us together to hear.

There are precise and demanding rules of telling, but it is
the voice's imagination and skill that carry the Spirit's message and intent, as God comes sounding through us. Each
human being is the best gift, the best story each can tell, the
only response to God's sigh and breath pouring into us and
bringing us to life. We hasten the coming of Truth, the fulfill-
ment of the promises spoken and clung to and of the dreams
sketched on scrolls whenever we take a deep breath and
begin: "Once upon a time..." Inherent in that beginning is the
prayer and fervent blessing: "May you come true and may
there be life everlasting where all creation lives happily ever
after. Amen."

Jon Sobrino once said there are two kinds of people in the
world: the ones who take life for granted and the ones who
don't. Crucifixion is the image, he continued, of those who
can't take life for granted. Perhaps there are only two kinds of
people who tell stories: those who take words for granted and
those who can't or won't because they believe and proclaim
that The Word dwells among us. They believe that we stand
on our words and, in a world where there is so much that is
an affront to life, they pledge to resist, to brace themselves
with stories and sign themselves, crossing word and flesh
again and again, responding amen to every story told that
nurtures truth and life in the world.

If God rests on the Sabbath to listen to our stories, then
perhaps heaven is nothing more than the place and the time
where all the stories are told. They are sung, honored and delighted in so that their truth echoes throughout the universe,
and is woven in and out of the stars—perhaps.

The stories must make us look at and face all the ragged
edges of life as well as attend to the details of loveliness, for

the truth embraces both sides of the hand. Long ago, I wrote the next two stories.

* I knew a man once. No one seemed to remember his name. He had just always been there. He sold balloons on a street corner in Washington, D.C., mostly at night. In the snow and rain and on windy days he stood there under his splotches of color, holding onto them, keeping them close to the earth. He didn't talk much and never asked you if you wanted one. He just stood there like he was reminding you of something even he couldn't remember well enough to put into words. Tall and black, white-haired and alone, the man belonged on that corner. During the day when he was often absent, the corner looked bleak and empty—crying out for his presence and his colors. The corner lived only at night. You weren't aware of it until there was nothing there to look at or to look for when you passed by.

    And now, the man comes no more to the corner. Someone said he died over the holidays. But when I come to the corner, he's still there. I remember. I see and know he still waits for someone to buy his balloons. And I wonder if there's any place that my presence fills up and makes whole, or whether I move so fast that there is no space that is touched so intimately and thoroughly by me that it is truly mine. And you—where's your space?

Years later I still remember and wonder about such things. Sometimes it is a small piece of reality standing out starkly that arrests attention and becomes a kernel of truth that becomes a question, then a story that questions. Other times it arrives in a dream, in a phrase overheard, or in thoughts that drift through while one is attending to something that is gloriously mundane. Out of myriad of sunbeams and dust motes, a few become shafts of insight and memory.

* Once upon a time I dreamed. In my dream I came to a planet of darkness. It didn't look like earth. It was full of music and laughter like chimes and air that carried echoes

in the background all around me, a background of shadows and immense stars.

Two children, a boy and a girl, were playing. Their arms, hands, legs, feet, all the skin of their bodies was etched and streaked with traces and intricate patterns of light that made them move like dancers, will-o-the-wisps in the twilight. They were playing—with stars and streaks of light. I watched, half-hidden, fascinated and wanting so desperately to play. They threw, faster and faster: the shafts and orbs and stars multiplying.

Unknowingly I stepped out. Great laughter. I was included in the game. Quick, in both directions, light, fire, delight. Then I dropped one, a lightning bolt, and it went right through my foot and pinned me to the ground. Incredible pain, terror, horror. They ran to me. "Forgive us. We are sorry. We forgot you were of earth." They took out the light and a scar formed white and silvery where it had entered my foot.

A realization: All those traces on their bodies, scars of light.

I spoke, "You are all so scarred."

"Yes. When we were young we dropped the stars a lot and couldn't hold onto the light. It's better now, reflexive, more natural."

"When you were young?" I asked. "How old are you?"

They laughed so easily, completely, freely. "We are only apprentices," they said, "That is all we can tell you about us. But we can share with you these three truths: Angels recognize the children of light from their scars. Stars don't fall, they are thrown in delight. And remember, light is always more powerful and dangerous than the dark, though light loves the dark. Remember."

I awoke, expecting to see a scar, a trace of light where I had dropped a flash of lightning on my foot. There was nothing, unless you looked *really* closely. Now the stars are my friends. And I remember and wonder... every time a star falls, lightning flashes, a scar on skin is noticed, a light falls on a face in a certain way...

Much later, I realized that my first gift from an Indian tribe had been a lightning bracelet, a gift for storytelling, the symbol of tellers in that native tradition. Since then, I have always wondered.

And finally, a look at the last things, a reflection at the end of a long day. The title of this story by Tony Cowan says it all: "By the Second Funeral of the Day."

✳ Michael's joyride ended when he crashed headfirst through the windshield as his Camaro hit the barrier. Michael. Age sixteen.

Kathleen died with her friends when their speeding car ended up wrapped around a sturdy lamp-post. Kathleen. Age twenty-one. Two funerals back-to-back.

How naked you all were, how vulnerable as you crowded into unfamiliar pews. Grief had stripped you raw, compelling your souls, stopping your tongues, making you human enough to effect a brief community, unaccustomed as you are. I did not use God to point a finger at the dead boy, as his sister feared I would. No. I pointed at you and asked what Michael had learned about love, about life, from you; what Kathleen had discovered of God because of you. Were sixteen or twenty-one years enough to have learned why God gave them life because you reminded them with your love?

You weren't expecting that. It showed in your faces. Reward-and-punishment is so much simpler.

But a well-dressed man grabbed my hand after he had received communion, halting the line behind him. "Thank you for the speech, Father," he sputtered, "but what are we going to do about these young men? What are we supposed to tell them? Today's youth!"

Jesus, was it hard for you to be swallowed with so much anger and frustration? Was it *his* Camaro?

By the second funeral of the day my chest was so swollen and tight that I crashed heart first through the ritual. Tony. Age thirty-one.

I see you, schoolgirl, with shock-frosted eyes.

I see you, mother, whose mind is shapeless gray.

I see you, front-row pall-bearer, fifteen years old,
>   you never took yo' black shades off
>   you got the hair-cut
>   you walk the block, got the style,
>   you got the suit an' the chains
>   you one mean bad dude
>   nobody gonna see you cry
>   behind them shades
>   cos you the man. Yeah.
You especially I wonder about.
God's house never looked so dark.

What are your shades protecting you from seeing here?

Departing from formula at the end (I am so desperate to reach you, to touch you somehow) I move from person to person across the front rows, placing one hand on your shoulder, the other over your heart, praying God's peace into you. When I come to you with the shades I press my palm into your heart a little firmer and I can feel it beating, now a little slower, a little harder. Opening my eyes I face the fear expressed by that well-dressed man at communion, the wild fear that says, "One of these young men might drive by the church, kill a preacher, get in good with the gang."

And now they know what I look like.

Opening my eyes, I see tears slipping under the rim of your impenetrable shades and my fear of you vanishes along with your cool. Even my crazy fear has to admit that you won't kill me now...not now you've let me hold your heart in my palm.

Will you now do this for each other? Not just at the curbside...not just at the graveside...not just at the catered lunch,...but for the rest of your lives? Will you touch your hand to someone's pain and feel his heart break free there?

Back in my room afterwards, I brush grief from my neck and shoulders with the feather of a hawk and press a crucifix into my heart to soak up excess pain. By the second funeral of the day, grief had stripped me raw, compelled my soul, stopped my tongue, made me human enough to effect a brief community, unaccustomed as I am.

I wasn't expecting that. Maybe it showed in my face. Life and death are so much simpler.

In the end, our stories must do so much more than give meaning, or hope or enduring grace in the face of life and death. They must make community, make amends, redeem and endear every human face to us. They must make us true and turn our bodies into quickened flesh that begins to tremble with resurrection even now in the midst of the tearing of severed hearts. Our stories must heed the Presence that hides in every breath, in every word and sound and silence, waiting to be found out and brought home. Our stories must ask the ancient question once again: Do you believe? We answer and so we tell stories, all our stories, saying simply "Yes!"

Resources

Eduardo Galeano, speech to the World Congress of Christian Communicators. A shortened version of this speech appeared in *Far East*, April 1996, pp. 2-3.
Elie Wiesel, Nobel Prize Acceptance Speech, *New York Times*, December 11, 1986.